YING KE • TIAN XIA

"中国式现代化的故事"丛书
张占斌　总主编

迎客天下

中国式现代化的黄山故事

中共黄山市委党校（黄山市行政学院）　编著

（汉英对照版）

·北京·
中央党校出版集团
国家行政学院出版社

出版说明

党的二十大报告指出，从现在起，中国共产党的中心任务就是团结带领全国各族人民全面建成社会主义现代化强国、实现第二个百年奋斗目标，以中国式现代化全面推进中华民族伟大复兴。习近平总书记在中央党校建校90周年庆祝大会暨2023年春季学期开学典礼上的讲话中首次创造性提出"为党育才、为党献策"的党校初心。紧扣党的中心任务，践行党校初心，中央党校出版集团国家行政学院出版社和中央党校（国家行政学院）中国式现代化研究中心特别策划"中国式现代化的故事"丛书，邀请地方党校（行政学院）、宣传部门、新闻媒体、行业企业等方面共同参与策划和组织编写，从不同层次、不同维度、不同视角讲述中国式现代化的地方故事、企业故事、产业故事，生动展示各个地区、各个领域在大力拓展中国式现代

Publication Instructions

The 20th CPC National Congress Report points out that, from this day forward, the central task of the CPC will be to lead the Chinese people of all ethnic groups in a concerted effort to realize the Second Centenary Goal of building China into a great modern socialist country in all respects and to advance the rejuvenation of the Chinese nation on all fronts through a Chinese path to modernization. In the speech at the 90th anniversary celebration of the founding of the Party School of the Central Committee of CPC (CCPS) and the opening ceremony of its spring semester of 2023, President Xi Jinping first creatively underlined the original mission for Party schools to cultivate talent for and contribute wisdom to the CPC. In line with the central task of the CPC and the original mission for Party schools, National Academy of Governance Press and the Chinese Modernization Research Center of CCPS (National Academy of Governance) have specially planned the series of books "The Story of Chinese Modernization", inviting local Party schools (administration institutes), publicity departments, news media, industry enterprises, and other aspects to jointly participate in the planning and organizing of the writing. The books will tell the local stories, enterprise stories, and industry stories of Chinese modernization from different levels, perspectives, and dimensions, vividly showcasing the innovative ideas, practices, systems, and culture in various regions and fields in the new journey of expanding Chinese modernization. It will present a magnificent historical narrative of the promotion of the rejuvenation of the Chinese

化新征程上的理念创新、实践创新、制度创新、文化创新等，精彩呈现当代中国以中国式现代化全面推进中华民族伟大复兴的宏大历史叙事，以讲好中国式现代化的故事来讲好中国故事。

该丛书力求体现这样几个突出特点：

其一，文风活泼，以白描手法代入鲜活场景。本丛书区别于一般学术论著或理论读物严肃刻板的面孔，以生动鲜活的题材、清新温暖的笔触、富有现场感的表达和丰富精美的图片，将各地方、企业推进中国式现代化建设的理论思考、战略规划、重要举措、实践路径等向读者娓娓道来，使读者在沉浸式的阅读体验中获得共鸣、引发思考、受到启迪。

其二，视野开阔，以小切口反映大主题。丛书中既有历史人文风貌、经济地理特质的纵深概述，也有改革创新举措、转型升级案例的细节剖解，既讲天下事，又讲身边事，以点带面、以小见大，用故事提炼经验，以案例支撑理论，从而兼顾理论厚度、思想深度、实践力度和情感温度。

其三，层次丰富，以一域之光映衬全域风采。丛书有开风气之先的上海气度，也有立开放潮头的南粤之声；有沉稳构筑首都经济圈的京津冀足音，也有聚力谱写东北全面振兴的黑吉辽篇章；有在长江三角洲区域一体化发展中厚积薄发的安徽样板，也有在成渝

nation on all fronts through a Chinese path to modernization, and better tell China's story to the world by better telling the story of Chinese modernization.

This series of books strives to embody the following prominent features:

First, the writing style is lively, using vivid descriptions to depict vivid scenes. This series of books differs from the serious and rigid face of general academic works or theoretical readings. With lively and vivid subjects, fresh and warm brushstrokes, expression of a sense of presence, and rich and exquisite images, it narrates the theoretical thinking, strategic planning, important measures, and practical paths of promoting construction of Chinese modernization by various regions and enterprises, allowing readers to resonate, think, and be inspired through immersive reading experiences.

Second, it has a broad vision and reflects major themes through small perspectives. The series of books includes both a deep overview of the historical and cultural characteristics and economic geography traits, as well as detailed analysis of reform and innovation measures and transformation and upgrading cases. It talks about both national affairs and local affairs, uses specific stories to extract experiences, supports theories with cases, and thus takes into account the thickness of theory, the depth of thought, the intensity of practice, and the warmth of emotions.

Third, it has rich levels, reflecting the regional brilliance against the backdrop of the overall picture. The series of books include the elegance of Shanghai, which leads the trend, and the voice of innovation and openness in Guangdong; the sound of Beijing, Tianjin, and Hebei, which steadily builds the capital economic zone, and the chapters of Heilongjiang, Jilin, and Liaoning that gather strength for the comprehensive revitalization of Northeast China; the Anhui model that accumulates strength and breakthroughs in the development of the Yangtze River Delta regional integration, and the practical exploration of

地区双城经济圈中走深走实的川渝实践；有生态高颜值、发展高质量齐头并进的云南画卷，也有以"数"为笔、逐浪蓝海的贵州答卷；有"强富美高"的南京路径，也有"七个新天堂"的杭州示范……。丛书还将陆续推出各企业、各行业的现代化故事，带读者领略中国式现代化的深厚底蕴、辽阔风光和壮美前景。

"中国式现代化的故事"丛书既是各地方、企业推进中国式现代化建设充满生机活力的形象展示，也是以地方、企业发展缩影印证中国式现代化理论科学性的多维解码。希望本丛书的出版，能够为各地方、企业搭建学习交流平台，将一地一域的现代化建设融入全面建设社会主义现代化国家的大局，步伐一致奋力谱写中国式现代化的历史新篇章。

国家行政学院出版社
"中国式现代化的故事"丛书策划编辑组

Chengdu-Chongqing economic zone; the Yunnan picture with high ecological value and simultaneous high-quality development, and the Guizhou paper that uses "numbers" as brushes to explore blue oceans; the development goal towards "strong economy, rich people, beautiful environment and a high degree of social civilization" in Nanjing, and the demonstration of construction of seven types of new paradise in Hangzhou... The series of books will also gradually launch the modernization stories of various enterprises and industries, allowing readers to appreciate the profound heritage, vast scenery, and magnificent prospects of Chinese modernization.

The series of books "The Story of Chinese Modernization" is not only a vibrant display of promoting construction of Chinese modernization by various regions and enterprises, but also a multi-dimensional decoding of the scientificity of Chinese modernization theory through the epitome of local and enterprise development. It is hoped that the publication of this series of books can provide a platform for learning and exchange for various regions and enterprises, integrate the modernization construction of single place and single region into the overall construction of a modern socialist country, and strive to write a new chapter in the history of Chinese modernization with consistent steps.

Planned and Editorial Team of
the series of books "The Story of Chinese Modernization",
National Academy of Governance Press

总　序

党的二十大擘画了全面建成社会主义现代化强国、以中国式现代化全面推进中华民族伟大复兴的宏伟蓝图。中国式现代化是前无古人的开创性事业，是强国建设、民族复兴的康庄大道。回顾过去，中国共产党带领人民艰辛探索、铸就辉煌，用几十年时间走完西方发达国家几百年走过的工业化历程，创造了经济快速发展和社会长期稳定的两大奇迹，实践有力证明了中国式现代化走得通、行得稳；面向未来，在以习近平同志为核心的党中央坚强领导下，各地方各企业立足各自的资源禀赋、区位优势和产业基础、发展规划，精心谋划、奋勇争先，在推进中国式现代化过程中将展现出一系列生动场景，一步一个脚印地把美好蓝图变为现实形态。

中国式现代化，是中国共产党领导的社会主义现

The General Prologue

The 20th CPC National Congress had planed the grand blueprint to build China into a great modern socialist country in all respects, and to advance rejuvenation of the Chinese nation on all fronts through a Chinese path to modernization. Chinese modernization is an unprecedented pioneering endeavor, which represents the grand path towards building a strong nation and achieving national rejuvenation. Looking back, we have led the people through arduous exploration and achieved brilliance, completing the industrialization process that took Western developed countries hundreds of years in just a few decades. We have created two miracles of rapid economic development and long-term social stability, proving that Chinese modernization is feasible and sustainable. Looking towards the future, under the strong leadership of the CPC Central Committee with Xi Jinping at the core, each region and enterprise will rely on their respective resources, geographical advantages, industrial foundations, and development plans to carefully plan and strive to be at the forefront. In the process of advancing Chinese modernization, a series of vivid scenes will be presented, step by step, transforming the beautiful blueprint into a tangible reality.

代化，既有各国现代化的共同特征，又有基于自己国情的中国特色。中国式现代化，是人口规模巨大的现代化，是全体人民共同富裕的现代化，是物质文明和精神文明相协调的现代化，是人与自然和谐共生的现代化，是走和平发展道路的现代化。这五个方面的中国特色，不仅深刻揭示了中国式现代化的科学内涵，也体现在不同地方、企业推进现代化建设可感可知可行的实际成果中。中国式现代化理论为地方、企业现代化的实践探索提供了不竭动力，地方、企业推进中国式现代化建设的成就也印证了中国式现代化道路行稳致远的时代必然。

为讲好中国式现代化的故事，更加全面、立体、直观地呈现中国式现代化的丰富内涵和万千气象，中央党校（国家行政学院）中国式现代化研究中心和中央党校出版集团国家行政学院出版社联合策划推出"中国式现代化的故事"丛书，展现各地方、企业等在着眼全国大局、立足地方实际、发挥自身优势，推进中国式现代化建设上的新突破新作为新担当，总结贯穿其中的完整准确全面贯彻新发展理念、构建新发展格局、推动高质量发展的新理念新方法新经验。我们希望该系列丛书一本一本的出下去，能够为各地更好推进中国式现代化建设以启迪和思考，为以中国式现代化全面推进中华民族伟大复兴凝聚更加巩固的思想

Chinese modernization is a socialist modernization under the leadership of the CPC that combines common features of modernization in various countries with Chinese characteristics based on its own national conditions. Chinese modernization is characterized by a large population, shared prosperity for all its people, the harmonious coordination of material and spiritual civilization, the harmonious coexistence of humans and nature, and the pursuit of peaceful development. These five aspects of Chinese characteristics not only reveal the scientific connotation of Chinese modernization, but also reflect tangible achievements in the modernization efforts of different regions and enterprises. The theory of Chinese modernization provides endless motivation for the practical exploration of modernization in different regions and enterprises, and the achievements of localities and enterprises in advancing construction of Chinese modernization confirm the inevitability of the steady and far-reaching path of Chinese modernization in this era.

To tell the story of Chinese modernization, and to showcase the rich connotations and diverse aspects of Chinese modernization more comprehensively, vividly, and intuitively, the Chinese Modernization Research Center of CCPS and National Academy of Governance Press have jointly planned and launched the series of books "The Story of Chinese Modernization". These books aim to demonstrate the new breakthroughs, achievements, and responsibilities of various regions, enterprises, etc., in promoting Chinese modernization, by focusing on the overall national situation, local realities, and

基础，为进一步推进中国式现代化的新实践、书写中国式现代化的新篇章汇聚磅礴力量。

中央党校（国家行政学院）
中国式现代化研究中心主任
2023 年 10 月

leveraging their own advantages. They also summarize and implement the new development concepts, new development patterns, and new ideas, methods, and experiences for promoting high-quality development. We hope that this series of books will be published one by one, to inspire and stimulate thinking, and to better promote construction of Chinese modernization in various regions. They will serve as a solid ideological foundation for the advancement of the rejuvenation of the Chinese nation on all fronts through a Chinese path to modernization. This will gather tremendous strength for further advancing new practices and writing new chapters of Chinese modernization.

Zhang Zhanbin
The chief director of
Chinese Modernization Research Center of CCPS
October, 2023

目 录

1 黄山　不止是山水

一座没有屋顶的徽州文化博物馆　　2

中国旅游从黄山出发　　10

2 心驰神往　人间仙境

黄山风景区　　20

皖南古村落：西递村和宏村　　32

古徽州文化旅游区　　38

3 人文徽州　底蕴深厚

徽派建筑　水墨画卷　　52

匠心文化　非遗传承　　70

王茂荫：《资本论》里提到的

　唯一的中国人　　88

CONTENTS

1 More than Mountain and River
An Open Museum of Huizhou Culture 3
Chinese Tourism Starts from Mount Huangshan 9

2 A Fascinating Wonderland
Mount Huangshan Scenic Area 21
Ancient Villages in Southern Anhui Province: Xidi Village
and Hongcun Village 31
Ancient Huizhou Cultural Tourism Area 37

3 Humanistic Huizhou with Rich and Profound Heritage
Huizhou-Style Architecture in Ink and Wash Paintings 53
Ingenious Culture, Inheritance of Intangible Cultural
Heritage 71
Wang Maoyin: the Only Chinese Mentioned in *Capital* 89

4 一江好水　一城秀美

"现代城市"到"秀美之城" 　　96

"新安江水"到"一江好水" 　　108

"环境良好"到中国"绿都" 　　118

5 茶乡山居　香飘万里

茶香四溢 　　132

"食"徽系美味　"宿"徽州美宿 　　140

各享其行　畅游徽州 　　150

6 和美乡村　宜居宜业

共同富裕惠村民 　　164

宜居宜业美村民 　　172

德治善治和村民 　　182

7 开放高地　迎客天下

大黄山世界级休闲度假康养旅游目的地 　　196

长三角一体化高质量发展 　　202

黄山："国际会客厅" 　　210

后记 　　222

4 Clean River　Beautiful City

    A Beautiful Modern City　　　　　　　　　　　　　97

    The Clean Water of Xin'an River　　　　　　　　109

    The Green City with Favourable Environment　　121

5 Dwelling in Tea Producing Villages with Fragrance Drifting for Thousands of Miles

    The Fragrance of Tea Fills the Air　　　　　　　　133

    Taste Huizhou Cuisine and Live in Huizhou Mansion　141

    Enjoy the Journey and Travel Freely in Huizhou　　151

6 Livable and Business-Friendly, Harmonious and Beautiful Countryside

    Common Prosperity Benefits Villagers　　　　　　165

    Livable and Business-Friendly Village Benefits Villagers　173

    Good Governance Through Moral Means Makes Villagers Harmonious　　183

7 An Opening-up Highland　Greeting the World

    The Grand Huangshan World-Class Leisure and Healthcare Tourism Destination　　197

    The High-Quality Integrated Development of the Yangtze River Delta　　203

    Huangshan: "the International Meeting Room"　　211

Epilogue　　　　　　　　　　　　　　　　　　　223

黄山
不止是山水

"五岳归来不看山,黄山归来不看岳",黄山冠绝天下、世界知名。黄山不仅是一座山,还是一座城。黄山市位于安徽省南部,辖三区(屯溪区、黄山区、徽州区)四县(歙县、休宁县、黟县、祁门县),总面积9807平方公里,户籍人口147万人。黄山市依托黄山、徽州两个顶流IP,发展"山水村夜",建设和美乡村,打造开放高地,入选中国十大秀美之城,全力推进大黄山世界级休闲度假康养旅游目的地,奋力谱写更加精彩的中国式现代化黄山篇章。

More than Mountain and River

"Trips to China's five great mountains render trips to other mountains unnecessary, and a trip to Mount Huangshan renders trips to the five great mountains unnecessary." The name of Mount Huangshan spreads the world and it is world famous. Huangshan is not only a mountain, but also a city. Huangshan City, located in the south of Anhui Province, has jurisdiction over three districts (Tunxi District, Huangshan District, Huizhou District) and four counties (Shexian County, Xiuning County, Yixian County, Qimen County), with a total area of 9,807 square kilometers and a registered population of 1.47 million. Relying on the two "hot IP" of Mount Huangshan and Huizhou, this city develops the new tourism coordinate system of mountains, waters, villages and night economy, and builds harmonious countrysides. It creates an open highland and has been selected as one of the top ten beautiful cities of China. Now the city tries every effort to build the Grand Huangshan world-class leisure and healthcare tourism destination, and tries to write a more wonderful chapter of Chinese modernization in Huangshan.

迎客天下
YING KE TIAN XIA

一座没有屋顶的徽州文化博物馆

　　黄山市的历史悠久，其文明的源头可以追溯到距今 5000 多年前。公元前 221 年，秦始皇统一中国后设立黟、歙两县为黄山域内最早的行政建置；隋唐设歙州；公元 1121 年，宋徽宗改歙州为徽州，辖歙县、休宁、黟县、绩溪、祁门、婺源六县；1987 年，撤徽州地区设地级黄山市。

黄山市城区夜景（宋雨晨　摄）
The night view of Huangshan City (Photo by Song Yuchen)

An Open Museum of Huizhou Culture

Huangshan City has a long history and its civilization can be traced back to more than 5,000 years ago. In 221 BC, the First Emperor of Qin unified the whole country. After that, Yixian and Shexian counties were established as the first administrative places in Huangshan region. In the Sui and Tang Dynasties, She Prefecture was established. In 1121, Emperor Huizong of the Song Dynasty changed She Prefecture to Huizhou, including six counties: Shexian County, Xiuning County, Yixian County, Jixi County, Qimen County and Wuyuan County. In 1987, Huangshan City, the prefecture-level city, replaced Huizhou.

The Huizhou culture of Huangshan City is profound. The whole city is like an open museum. Huizhou has experienced three great population migrations in its history. The fusion and symbiosis of Zhongyuan culture, Confucian culture and Shanyue culture have formed the unique Huizhou culture, spanning across various fields like economics, history, philosophy, medicine, science and technology, arts, etc. Literature shaped trends, scholarship formed factions, commerce formed guilds, and vulgarity evolved into elegance, giving rise to Xin'an philosophy, Xin'an medicine, Xin'an painting school, Huizhou carving school and so on. Influential thinkers and cultural masters such as Zhu Xi, Dai Zhen, Hu Shi, Tao Xingzhi and Huang Binhong emerged.

迎客天下
YING KE TIAN XIA

  黄山市徽州文化底蕴深厚，犹如一座没有屋顶的博物馆。徽州历史上经历过 3 次人口大迁徙，中原文化、儒家文化、山越文化在此融合共生，形成了独树一帜的徽州文化。其涵盖经济、历史、哲学、医学、科技、艺术等诸多领域，文成风、学成派、商成帮、俗成雅，孕育了新安理学、新安医学、新安画派、徽派雕刻等诸多文化流派，产生了朱熹、戴震、胡适、陶行知、黄宾虹等思想巨人和文化巨匠，演绎了"无

珠算进课堂（樊成柱　摄）
The abacus calculation has been introduced into class (Photo by Fan Chengzhu)

The legend of Huizhou merchants—"No town without Huizhou merchants", came to life. With 5 intangible cultural heritages of humanity, 310 traditional Chinese villages, 8,000 cultural relics, and millions of documents, the whole city is exactly an open museum without the roof. Here, to experience the charm of Huizhou and feel the history, one can understand China better.

The ideas, humanistic spirit, moral norms, and traditional virtues such as love, honesty, justice, harmony, etc. in Huizhou culture, have a deep influence on people's values, daily words and deeds, as well as the social production and life.

The method of abacus calculation is a method of numerical calculation using an abacus as a tool. Cheng Dawei sorted out the abacus calculation formula, standardized the abacus calculation operation method, and collected the great achievements of the abacus calculation in the past. Finally he compiled and published *The Direct Calculation Law System*, which realized the transition of Chinese arithmetic from the planning era to the abacus calculation era.

In 2008, abacus calculation (Cheng Dawei–abacus calculation method) was listed in the second batch of national intangible cultural heritage list. In the modern age of information technology, the glory days of the abacus calculation seem to be fading away. However, there is a school named after Cheng Dawei as Dawei Primary School in his hometown—Huangshan City. Dawei Primary School

徽不成镇"的徽商传奇。5项人类非物质文化遗产、310处中国传统村落、8000处文化遗存、百万件文书文献,整个城市宛如一座没有屋顶的博物馆。在这里,你可以感悟徽州、触摸历史、读懂中国。

徽州文化中蕴含的思想观念、人文精神、道德规范,以及讲仁爱、守诚信、崇正义、尚和合等传统美德,更是深深影响着人们的价值观念、日常言行和社会生产生活。

珠算是以算盘为工具进行数字计算的一种方法。程大位整理编定珠算口诀,规范珠算运算方法,集历代珠算之大成编撰出版《直指算法统宗》,实现了中国算术从筹算时代向珠算时代过渡。

2008年,珠算(程大位珠算法)列入第二批国家级非物质文化遗产名录。在现代信息技术时代,珠算的光辉年代似乎已经渐行渐远,但是在程大位的故乡黄山市有一所以程大位的名字命名的学校——大位小学。大位小学将珠算非遗纳入课程设置和课后服务,组织学生参观珠算博物馆,学习珠算文化,激发学生学习珠算的兴趣。

珠算成为孩子们启智的好帮手,广泛地应用在小学数学教学中。祁门县的阊江小学从1992年开始进行珠心算教学实践工作,推出课间珠算操"阊小娃",唱词是珠心算口诀,珠心算文化符号深深烙印在学生认

has incorporated the abacus calculation into its curriculum and after-school services, and organized students to visit the abacus museum, learn the abacus calculation culture, and stimulate their interest in the abacus calculation.

Abacus calculation has become a good assistant for children to enlighten their minds and is widely used in primary school mathematics teaching. Chang Jiang Primary School in Qimen County began to carry out mental abacus calculation teaching practice in 1992, and launched the abacus calculation exercise "Chang Xiaowa" during recess. The chant is the mental abacus calculation formula, and the cultural symbol of mental abacus calculation is deeply imprinted in students' cognition. In 2024, Chang Jiang Primary School opened the abacus calculation intangible culture heritage experience hall. The experience hall is divided into the abacus calculation history hall, the abacus calculation exhibition hall and the abacus calculation experience area. Abacus calculation experience area sets up abacus painting and rubbing, DIY abacus, dice bead translation, dialing the hand to tell the time, mental abacus calculation display and other activities. "It's amazing!" Students in the experience issued a highly praise, scrambling to experience the abacus calculation works of rubbing and rolling printing. Through experiencing the vivid works, the students will be engraved with the culture in their hearts. The ancient abacus calculation culture shines brightly in the classroom, and Cheng Dawei abacus calculation method has

迎客天下
YING KE TIAN XIA

知里。2024年阊江小学珠算非遗体验馆开馆，体验馆分为珠算历史厅、珠算展示厅和珠算体验区。珠算体验区设置了珠算绘画拓印、自制算盘、掷骰子珠译数、拨指针说时间、珠算心算展示等活动。"太神奇了！"学生在体验中发出赞叹，争先恐后地体验珠算作品拓印滚印，一幅幅生动的作品将历经千秋的算筹文化植根于同学们的心中。古老的珠算文化在课堂里绽放光彩，程大位珠算法得到了创新性地传承。

　　清道光年间，黟县人胡文照在修缮祖居时，为方便路人挑担、推车、行走，主动将正屋墙角削去三分、

九思堂（程向阳　摄）

The Jiusi Hall (Photo by Cheng Xiangyang)

been innovatively inherited.

During Daoguang period of Qing Dynasty, Hu Wenzhao from Yixian County, took the initiative to cut three points off the corner of the main house and take a step back from the attic on the street, when he was repairing his ancestral home. He inscribed "taking a back step" on the door for warning later generations of the way of treating people—"Cut straight into a circle to be convenient for others."

Huangshan City summarizes and promotes the mediation work method with the six words—listen, reason, persuade, borrow, withdraw, harmony as the main connotation. This creates the brand of social governance characteristics of "taking a back step". More than 98% of contradictions and disputes are resolved below the township (street). Huangshan City becomes one of the first batch of national urban social governance modernization pilot qualified cities.

Culture thrives because of continuity, and tradition endures because of innovation. To dig the value of Huizhou culture deeply, to tell Chinese stories well, and to polish the cultural brand, can expand the communication power and the influence of traditional Huizhou culture.

Chinese Tourism Starts from Mount Huangshan

"There is no mountain that can compare to the emblem of Mount Huangshan at home and abroad. Mount Huangshan

迎客天下
YING KE TIAN XIA

阁楼临街后退一步,并在门额上题下"作退一步想",告诫后代子孙"裁直为圆,方便他人"的待人处事之道。

黄山市总结推广以"听、理、劝、借、退、和"六字为主要内涵的调解工作法,打造"作退一步想"社会治理特色品牌。98%以上的矛盾纠纷在乡镇(街道)以下得到化解,成为首批全国市域社会治理现代化试点合格城市。

文化因赓续而繁荣兴盛,传统因创新而历久弥新。深入挖掘徽州文化的时代价值,讲好中国故事,擦亮文化品牌,扩大传播力和影响力。

中国旅游从黄山出发

"薄海内外,无如徽之黄山。登黄山,天下无山,观止矣!"400多年前,明代大旅行家徐霞客两次登临黄山,因念黄山"生平奇览"而如此赞叹。

1979年夏天,改革开放的总设计师邓小平以75岁高龄徒步登上黄山之巅,发表了著名的"黄山谈话"。

邓小平强调,这里是发展旅游的好地方,要有点雄心壮志,把黄山的牌子打出去!旅社建筑要搞得古色古香,将来要装冷风机。宾馆要设小卖部。"你们的祁红、绿茶世界有名,可以搞小包装,一两、二两的。

stands tall as a world-renowned peak, unmatched in its grandeur." admired by Xu Xiake more than 400 years ago, a great traveler in the Ming Dynasty. He visited Mount Huangshan twice and praised it greatly.

In the summer of 1979, Deng Xiaoping, the chief architect of reform and opening-up, climbed to the top of Mount Huangshan on foot at the age of 75 and delivered the famous "Huangshan Speech".

Deng Xiaoping said that this is a prime location for developing tourism. Be ambitious and promote the brand of Mount Huangshan! The hotel building should be antique and equipped with cooling fans in the future. The hotels will also establish concession stands to sell the famous black and green tea in small, beautiful packages. Additionally, Deng Xiaoping proposed promoting Anhui's paper, ink, pens, and inkstones through well-packaged products to earn foreign exchange. He also recommended creating high-quality photo albums featuring Mount Huangshan scenery and producing sets of postcards for tourists to purchase as souvenirs. These specialty items can be sold at commissaries at international prices, presenting significant business opportunities.

"Your capital is the mountain," Deng stated, "This region is wealthy and has the potential to become one of the most prosperous areas in the country." "It is not feasible for the income of 900 million people to develop at an equal rate. There will always be regions that experience prosperity before others, and individuals within those regions who

迎客天下
YING KE TIAN XIA

包装一定要很漂亮。""安徽的纸、墨、笔、砚,也要搞好包装,赚外汇。还要搞些好的黄山风景照片、画册,搞一套黄山风景明信片,让游客买去做纪念。小卖部卖这些特产,定出国际价格,大有买卖可做。"

邓小平指出:"你们的资本就是山。""你们的物产很丰富,这里将是全国最富的地方之一。""9亿人口的收入平均发展是不可能的,总是有的地区先富起来,一个地区总是有一部分人先富起来。旅游收入的外汇要与地方分成,开创时国家要投点资。"

邓小平的"黄山谈话"发出了黄山乃至中国现代旅游发展的动员令,拉开中国旅游业发展的大幕,掀开了黄山旅游发展新篇章。

随着旅游业快速发展,游客人数大量增加。当时的旅游基础设施尚不完善,尤其是在天都峰、莲花峰、始信峰等热门景点,游人集中、游览面积狭小,生态承载力受到严峻挑战。黄山风景区管理部门从"海洋休渔期"和"封山育林"的实践中受到启发,"为啥不让黄山的山峰也能歇一歇?"这一设想随后创造性地演化为"景点封闭轮休"新理念,并于1987年10月进入实施阶段,开始对始信峰实行封闭轮休。经过近两年的轮休,始信峰植物种类和生物量都呈现大幅增长,生态环境得到明显改善。随后,天都峰等景点也都陆续推广此方法,每个轮休期为3年至5年。2005年起,

achieve wealth first. The revenue generated from tourism should be shared with local governments, and it is essential for our country to initially invest some capital into these areas."

Deng Xiaoping's "Huangshan Speech" issued a mobilizing order for the modern tourism development of Mount Huangshan and even China, thus unveiling the curtain of China's tourism development and opening a new chapter in the development of Mount Huangshan tourism.

With the rapid development of tourism, the number of tourists has increased. At that time, the tourism infrastructure was not yet fully developed, especially at popular attractions such as Tiandu Peak, Lotus Peak, and Shixin Peak, where tourists flocked and the visiting area was small, posing a serious challenge to the ecological carrying capacity. The management department of Mount Huangshan Scenic Area was inspired by the practice of "ocean fishing ban" and "forest protection", and came up with the idea of "why not let the peaks of Mount Huangshan rest for a while?" This creative idea later evolved into the new concept of "scenic spot closure and rest period", which entered the implementation stage in October 1987 and began with the closure and restoration of Shixin Peak. After nearly two years of rest, the plant species and biomass of Shixin Peak showed a significant increase, and the ecological environment was restored significantly. Subsequently, Tiandu Peak and other scenic spots also introduced this method, with each rest period lasting 3 to 5 years. Since 2005, Mount Huangshan

迎客天下
YING KE TIAN XIA

黄山风景区对天都峰、莲花峰和西海大峡谷每年实行冬季封闭维护。2014年,"黄山景点封闭轮休"被列为中国履行《生物多样性公约》第五次国家报告的典型案例,由联合国环境规划署向全球发布,高度肯定了黄山以"封闭轮休"探索世界遗产保护管理和可持续发展过程中汇聚的智慧。

1996年11月,黄山旅游发展股份有限公司成立并成功上市,"黄山旅游"同时登陆A股、B股证券市场,成为中国第一只完整意义上的旅游概念股。

2022年2月,安徽省发布《皖南国际文化旅游示范区"十四五"建设发展规划》,首次明确提出"大

黄山市风光(程向阳 摄)
The scenery of Huangshan City (Photo by Cheng Xiangyang)

Scenic Area has closed and maintained Tiandu Peak, Lotus Peak, and the West Sea Grand Canyon every winter. In 2014, "Mount Huangshan Scenic Spot closure and rest period" was listed as a typical case in "the Fifth National Report on China's Implementation of *the Convention on Biological Diversity*" and released to the world by the United Nations Environment Programme (UNEP). It highly commended the wisdom that Mount Huangshan has accumulated in exploring the protection and management of world heritage sites and sustainable development through the practice of "closure and rest period".

In November 1996, Huangshan Tourism Development Co., Ltd. was established and successfully listed on the stock exchange, and "Huangshan Tourism" simultaneously listed on both the A-share and B-share stock markets, becoming China's first tourism concept stock.

In February 2022, Anhui Province released *The Fourteenth Five-year Plan for the Construction and Development of the Southern Anhui International Cultural and Tourism Demonstration Zone*, in which the concept of the "Grand Huangshan" was first explicitly proposed. Huangshan, Chizhou, Xuancheng, and Anqing have broken through the boundaries of their respective municipalities to unify in creating the "Grand Huangshan" super IP.

Huangshan has established friendly relationships with Swiss Jungfrau, Greek Lesvos, American Yosemite, Canadian Banff and other overseas sites on *the World Heritage List* and

黄山"概念。黄山、池州、宣城、安庆打破市域界限，统一打造"大黄山"超级大IP。

黄山已与瑞士少女峰、希腊莱斯沃斯、美国优胜美地、加拿大班芙等被列入《世界遗产名录》的地方和世界地质公园缔结友好关系；参与制定（修订）《全球可持续旅游目的地标准》《全球酒店业与旅游经营商可持续发展指南》并向全球发布。"可持续发展""卓越式发展"等黄山经验被联合国教科文组织、世界旅游组织等宣传推广，黄山的国际知名度、美誉度和影响力不断提升。

黄山，不止是山水。黄山市依托黄山、徽州两个顶流IP，打开"Z世代"与徽州文化的情感通道，推动山水"年轻化"、文化当代化、美食国际化，讲好中国式现代化的黄山故事。

World Geoparks; participated in the formulation (revision) of *the Guidelines for Sustainable Tourism Destinations Globally* and *the Guidelines for Sustainable Development of Hotels and Travel Agents Globally* and released them to the world. The Huangshan experience of sustainable and excellent development has been promoted by the UNESCO, the World Tourism Organization and other organizations. Huangshan's international recognition, reputation and influence have been steadily enhanced.

Huangshan offers more than just mountains and rivers. Leveraging the two "hot IP" of Mount Huangshan and Huizhou, Huangshan City has established an emotional connection with Generation Z and Huizhou culture. It promotes a youthful landscape, contemporary culture and international cuisine, and narrates the story of Chinese modernization in Huangshan.

心驰神往
人间仙境

　　黄山是世界名山、中国名片。黄山市拥有12处国家级重点风景名胜区、自然保护区、森林公园、地质公园,53家A级以上景区,其中5A级3家、4A级21家、3A级以下29家,以及310处国家级传统村落、492处省级传统村落、4072处历史建筑。其中黄山风景区、西递宏村、古徽州文化旅游区,是黄山市现有的3家5A级景区。

2

A Fascinating
Wonderland

    Mount Huangshan is a globally renowned mountain and serves as a prominent symbol of China. Huangshan City boasts 12 national key scenic spots, nature reserves, forest parks, and geological parks. Additionally, there are 53 scenic spots above A-level, including 3 at the 5A-level, 21 at the 4A-level, 29 below 3A-level. The city also features 310 national traditional villages, 492 provincial traditional villages, and 4,072 historical buildings. Notably, Mount Huangshan Scenic Area, Xidi and Hongcun villages, and Ancient Huizhou Cultural Tourism Area stand out as the three existing 5A-level scenic spots in Huangshan City.

迎客天下
YING KE TIAN XIA

黄山风景区

黄山风景区是全国现有的四处世界文化与自然双遗产之一，黄山被联合国教科文组织列入《世界文化与自然遗产名录》："黄山，在中国历史上文学艺术的鼎盛时期（公元16世纪中叶的'山水'风格）曾受到广泛的赞誉，以'震旦国中第一奇山'而闻名。今天，黄山以其壮丽的景色——生长在花岗岩石上的奇松和浮现在云海中的怪石而著称。对于从四面八方来到这个风景胜地的游客、诗人、画家和摄影家而言，黄山具有永恒的魅力。"

自然景观

黄山以奇松、怪石、云海、温泉、冬雪"五绝"著称于世，拥有"天下第一奇山"之称。

黄山名松上百株，其中黄山迎客松为黄山的形象代表，屹立在黄山风景区玉屏楼的青狮石旁，海拔1670米处。游客到此，顿时游兴倍增，纷纷摄影留念，引以为幸。

黄山已被命名的怪石有120多处，其形态各异，点缀在波澜壮阔的黄山峰海中。黄山怪石从不同的位置，在不同的天气观看，可谓"横看成岭侧成峰，远近高低各不同"。它们形态别致，或大或小，争相竞秀，意

Mount Huangshan Scenic Area

Mount Huangshan Scenic Area is one of the four existing World Cultural and Natural Heritage sites in China. Mount Huangshan was listed by UNESCO in *the World Cultural and Natural Heritage List*: "Mount Huangshan, which was widely praised in China's literary and artistic heyday (the landscape style of the mid-16th century) as 'the first wonder of the Celestial Empire', is today renowned for its magnificent scenery—the pine trees that grow on granite rocks and the bizarre rocks that emerge from the sea of clouds. For visitors, poets, painters, and photographers who come from all over the world to this scenic spot, Mount Huangshan has eternal charm."

Natural Landscape

Mount Huangshan is renowned for its "five wonders": peculiar pines, extraordinary rocks, sea of clouds, hot spring, and winter snow. It is widely acclaimed as the foremost marvelous mountain in the world.

There are numerous renowned pine trees in Mount Huangshan, among which the Guest-Greeting Pine in Mount Huangshan stands out as the iconic symbol of the area. It is situated next to the Qingshi Stone of Yuping Building in Mount Huangshan Scenic Area, at an elevation of 1,670 meters. As tourists arrive at this site, their excitement is heightened. They capture moments through photographs as

迎客天下
YING KE TIAN XIA

黄山飞来石（樊成柱　摄）
The Flying Stone (Photo by Fan Chengzhu)

趣无穷。有的酷似珍禽异兽，有的形同各种物品，有的又以历史故事、神话传说而命名。如"飞来石"是一块重约360吨的巨石，赫然耸立在一块长12～15米、宽8～10米的岩石平台上，形态奇特令人惊叹不已，两大岩石之间的接触面很小，上面的巨石似从天外飞来，故名"飞来石"。

自古黄山云成海，是云雾之乡，其瑰丽壮观的"云海"以美、胜、奇、幻享誉古今，一年四季皆可观，尤以冬季景最佳。依云海分布方位，全山有东海、南

mementos and feel privileged for having had this experience.

More than 120 strange rocks in Mount Huangshan have been named, whose shapes are varied and scattered among the mountains. The strange rocks of Huangshan can be seen from different angles and in different weather conditions, which can be described as "Viewed from the front, It's a ridge; from the side, a peak. From near or far, high or low, each view is unique." They are unique in shape, some large and some small, competing to show off their beauty, with endless interest. Some resemble rare birds and animals, some resemble various items, and some are named after historical stories and legends. "Flying Stone", a huge rock weighing about 360 tons, stands on a rock platform that is about 12~15 meters long and 8~10 meters wide, with a bizarre shape that amazes visitors. The contact area between the two rocks is very small, and the upper rock seems to have flown in from sky, hence its name "Flying Stone".

Since ancient times, Mount Huangshan has been known as the land of clouds, with clouds forming a sea. Its magnificent and spectacular "sea of clouds" is renowned for beauty, magnificence, uniqueness, and mystery throughout the ages, and can be viewed throughout the year, with the winter scenery being the best. According to the distribution of the sea of clouds, the whole mountain has the East Sea, the South Sea, the West Sea, the North Sea and Tianhai. There are more than 200 days of cloudy weather in Mount Huangshan every year, and sea of clouds will form when

迎客天下
YING KE TIAN XIA

黄山云海（樊成柱　摄）
The sea of clouds in Mount Huangshan (Photo by Fan Chengzhu)

海、西海、北海和天海。黄山一年之中有云雾的天气达 200 多天，水汽升腾或雨后雾气未消，就会形成云海。红树铺云是黄山深秋罕见的奇景，成片的红叶浮在云海之上。北海双剪峰是黄山的又一奇景，当云海挣脱两侧山峰的约束，从两峰之间流出，向下倾泻。

黄山温泉古称汤泉，源出海拔 850 米的紫云峰下，水质以含重碳酸为主，可饮可浴。传说轩辕黄帝就是在此沐浴七七四十九日得以返老还童、羽化飞升的，故又被誉为"灵泉"。黄山温泉由紫云峰下喷涌而出，与桃花峰隔溪，是游客经由黄山大门进入黄山的第一

water vapor rises or mist remains after a rainy day. Red trees covering in clouds—red leaves floating on the sea of clouds is a rare sight in late autumn in Mount Huangshan. The Double Scissors Peak of the North Sea is another scenic spot in Mount Huangshan, where the cloud flows between the two peaks after being constrained by the surrounding mountains, cascading downwards.

The Hot Spring of Mount Huangshan is also known as Tangquan. It originates from the foot of Ziyun Peak at an altitude of 850 meters. The water is mainly composed of heavy carbonate, which can be drunk and used to bath in. Legend has it that the Huangdi bathed here for 49 days, which made him return to his youth and ascend to heaven. Therefore, it is also known as "Spiritual Spring". The Hot Spring emerges from the base of Ziyun Peak and is across the creek from Taohua Peak. It is the first stop for visitors who enter Mount Huangshan through the main entrance. The Hot Spring produces about 400 tons of water per day and never stops flowing. The water temperature stays around 42 degrees Celsius all year round, making it a high-altitude hot spring. The Hot Spring has certain effects on certain diseases of the digestive, nervous, cardiovascular, metabolic, and locomotor systems.

Mount Huangshan often snows in winter, not only with a lower average temperature, but also due to its high elevation, often resulting in a sight of snow and rime covering mountains. In winter, Mount Huangshan is "a world of glass" and "a crystal palace" with snow-covered paths,

黄山冬雪（黄跃明　摄）

The winter snow in Mount Huangshan (Photo by Huang Yueming)

站。温泉每天的出水量在 400 吨左右，常年不息，水温常年在 42 度左右，属高山温泉。黄山温泉对消化、神经、心血管、新陈代谢、运动等系统的某些病症均有一定的疗效。

黄山冬季常下雪，不仅平均气温较低，而且由于黄山地势高耸，经常出现大雪、雾凇覆盖黄山的景观。冬日黄山"处处路通琉璃界，时时身在水晶宫"，有银装素裹的冬雪、晶莹剔透的雾凇、绚丽夺目的日出、磅礴壮阔的云海、清新润肺的空气。

文化遗产

黄山因轩辕黄帝和容成子、浮丘公来此炼丹、得道升天的仙道故事而得名。汉末，道教创立、佛教东传，黄山便成了道教和佛教相中的名山之一，众多

and with white snow, crystal rime, magnificent sunrises, vast sea of clouds, and a refreshing atmosphere.

Cultural Heritage

Mount Huangshan got its name from the legend that Huangdi, Rong Chengzi, and Fu Qiugong came here to refine elixir and ascend to heaven. During the late Han Dynasty, Taoism was founded and Buddhism was introduced to the east. Mount Huangshan became one of the famous mountains favored by both Taoism and Buddhism. Many famous "immortals" and monks came here and were so attracted by the scenery that they didn't want to leave, either to practice Taoism or to build temples. Many peaks with names related to the immortal stories mentioned above, such as Xuanyuan Peak, Fuqiu Peak, and some peaks named as Xiandu Peak, Daoren Peak, and Wangxian Peak, can still be found in the ancient Taoist books that have been passed down for over thousands of years and had a profound influence. The earliest Taoist temples established in Mount Huangshan are Fuqiu Temple and Jiulong Temple.

The cliff rock carvings of Mount Huangshan are a testament to the mountain civilization and diverse humanistic aspirations of different eras, and have significant historical, artistic, and scientific value. There are currently 352 inscriptions registered, which are mainly distributed in the core scenic areas, such as Hot Spring, Yuping, the North Sea, Yungu, and Songgu, with an inscription area exceeding 2,000 square meters. The inscription dates range from the

迎客天下
YING KE TIAN XIA

"名仙"高僧纷至沓来、流连忘返,或修炼,或建寺庙。唐代道教流传千年、影响深广的旧籍中至今还留有许多与上述神仙故事有关的峰名,如轩辕峰、浮丘峰,以及仙都、道人、望仙诸峰。道教在黄山建立较早的道观有浮丘观、九龙观等。

黄山摩崖石刻群是山岳文明、不同时代人文旨趣的见证,具有重要的历史、艺术和科学价值。现登记在册的题刻有352处,主要分布在温泉、玉屏、北海、云谷、松谷等核心游览区,题刻面积超过2000平方米。题刻年代从唐代延续至近现代,内容丰富,书艺精湛,篆

黄山摩崖石刻(程向阳 摄)
The cliff rock carvings of Mount Huangshan (Photo by Cheng Xiangyang)

Tang Dynasty to the modern times, with rich content and exquisite calligraphy, including seal script, official script, running script, and cursive script. Among them, the oldest are calligraphic works by the poet of Tang Dynasty Li Bai, such as "Ming Xian Quan" and "Xi Bei Quan". The largest inscription is the one engraved during the Republic of China period, which reads "Ride across the vast East Sea and ascend high to behold peace and tranquility." The single character is 6 meters in diameter, and the vertical stroke of " 平 " is 9.4 meters long. Through these cliff rock carvings, one cannot help but feel the charm and elegance of Chinese landscape culture with its distinctive national style.

Mount Huangshan has become the subject that countless poets praise and painters depict. Over the course of 1,200 years from the Tang Dynasty to the late Qing Dynasty, countless artistic works have been left, including more than 20,000 poems praising Mount Huangshan. These poems, songs and essays have endowed Mount Huangshan with a cultural soul, such as Li Bai's "Mount Huangshan stands tall with four thousand rens, boasting thirty-two lotus-like peaks." Xu Xiake's *Mount Huangshan Diary*, Yuan Mu's *Mount Huangshan Tour Record* and others. The legend about Huangdi refining elixir has endured to the present day. In ancient times, Huangdi, a tribal leader in the Yellow River basin, dispatched Fu Qiugong on a three-year journey to find an ideal location for refining elixir in pursuit of immortality and benevolence towards his people. Upon completion of his

书、隶书、行书、草书诸体皆备。其中年代最久的为唐代诗人李白手迹"鸣弦泉"、"洗杯泉";最大的题刻为民国时期所题"立马空东海、登高望太平",单字字径6米,"平"字一竖达9.4米。通过这些摩崖石刻,可感受到具有浓郁民族特色的中国山水文化的意趣与逸致。

黄山成为无数诗人咏叹、画家描绘的对象。从盛唐到晚清的1200年间留下了不可胜数的艺术作品,仅赞美黄山的诗词,现在可以查到的就有两万多首,这些诗词歌赋赋予黄山文化的灵魂。如李白的"黄山四千仞,三十二莲峰",徐霞客的《游黄山日记》,袁牧的《游黄山记》等。黄帝炼丹的故事流传至今:远古时代黄河流域的部落首领黄帝,为了长生不老、多为百姓办好事而炼制仙丹,便派遣浮丘公寻找适合炼丹的地方。浮丘公游历了3年后向黄帝推荐了黄山(当时的黟山)。黄帝被黄山的美景深深吸引,确认这里就是他寻找已久的炼丹圣地,并与弟子容成子在黄山之巅搭建炼丹炉,开始了漫长而艰辛的炼丹过程,最终炼成仙丹,黄帝也成了一名真正的仙人。黟山从此改名黄山,黄山72峰中就有炼丹峰、浮丘峰。有关黄山的艺术作品的体裁和内容都十分丰富,体现黄山俊美恬静的黄山画派,更是成为黄山文化中的一颗璀璨明珠。黄山哺育了各个时代的许多艺术家,艺术家们又赋予了黄山艺术生命。

quest, Fu Qiugong recommended Yishan Mountain (known today as Mount Huangshan) to Huangdi. He was deeply attracted by the beautiful scenery of Mount Huangshan, confirming that this was the long-sought sacred place for refining elixir. He then built an alchemy furnace with his disciple Rong Chengzi on the summit of Mount Huangshan, and began a long and arduous process of refining elixir. In the end, he succeeded in creating elixir, and Huangdi became a true immortal. From then on, Yishan Mountain was renamed Mount Huangshan, and the Alchemy Peak and the Fuqiu Peak are included in Mount Huangshan's 72 peaks. The genre and content of artworks about Mount Huangshan are extremely diverse. The Mount Huangshan school of painting reflects the elegant and serene beauty of Mount Huangshan. It has become a brilliant pearl in Huangshan culture. Mount Huangshan has nurtured many artists of different eras, and the artists have endowed Mount Huangshan with the vitality of art.

Ancient Villages in Southern Anhui Province: Xidi Village and Hongcun Village

The representatives of the ancient villages in southern Anhui, Xidi and Hongcun villages, are witnesses to ancient human civilization, typical works of traditional architecture, and brilliant examples of harmony between man and nature, and were listed on *the World Cultural Heritage List* in 2000.

迎客天下
YING KE TIAN XIA

皖南古村落：西递村和宏村

皖南古村落的代表——西递村、宏村是人类古老文明的见证，传统建筑的典型作品，人和自然结合的光辉典范，2000年被列入《世界文化遗产名录》。

西递村

全村有14—19世纪的祠堂3幢、牌坊1座、保存完好的明清古民居建筑224幢（其中124幢列入全国重点文物保护单位）。徽派建筑错落有致，大量的砖、木、石雕等艺术佳作点缀其间。西递村整体呈船形，四面环山，99条高墙深巷使游客如置身迷宫。村落以一条纵向的街道和两条沿溪的道路为主要骨架，构成东向为主、南北延伸的村落街巷系统。所有街巷均以黟县青石铺地，古建筑为木结构，砖墙维护，木雕、石雕、砖雕丰富多彩，巷道、溪流、建筑布局相宜。村落空间变化韵味有致，建筑色调朴素淡雅，体现了皖南古村落的人们在人居环境营造方面的杰出才能和成就。

西递的楹联折射出徽州人的家规家训和生活状态，通过这些楹联能发现传统徽州的良好家风。康熙年间建造的履福堂，厅堂题为"孝悌传家根本，诗书经世文章""读书好营商好效好便好，创业难守成难知难不难"的对联，显示出儒商本色。

Xidi Village

The village has 3 ancestral halls from the 14th to 19th century, 1 archway, and 224 well-preserved ancient residential buildings of the Ming and Qing dynasties (124 of which are listed as national key cultural relics protection units). The Huizhou-style architecture is arranged in a harmonious manner, with a large number of brick, wood, and stone carvings adorning the area. The village is shaped like a boat, surrounded by mountains on all sides, and its 99 high walls and narrow alleys make visitors feel as if they were in a maze. The village is mainly composed of a longitudinal street and two roads along the creek, forming a street and lane system oriented eastward and extending north and south. All lanes are paved with black slate from Yixian County, and the ancient buildings are made of wood with brick walls for maintenance. The wood carvings, stone carvings, and brick carvings are rich and colorful. The layout of the alleys, creeks, and buildings is appropriate. The spatial changes of the village are full of charm, and the architectural tones are simple and elegant. This shows the outstanding talent and achievements of the people from southern Anhui ancient villages in creating human living environments.

The couplets in Xidi Village reflect the family rules and morals of the people, and by studying them, one can discover the good family traditions. The Lvfu Hall built during the Kangxi period reveals the essence of a Confucian merchant by displaying a pair of couplets inscribed on the hall,

西递村（樊成柱　摄）
Xidi Village (Photo by Fan Chengzhu)

宏村

宏村位于黄山市黟县境内，以其独特的徽派建筑和美丽的自然风光而闻名，被誉为"画里的乡村"。

宏村宛若一头斜卧山前溪边的青牛，是一座"牛形村落"，保留了完好的明清古建筑群，其中承启楼和卧牛山民居尤为著名。承启楼建于明朝，已有400多年历史，是宏村最古老的建筑之一，以其高墙大院、马头翘角和白墙黛瓦的典型徽派风格著称。卧牛山民居则是清代的古民居，擅长木雕、石雕等细节装饰工艺。

宏村有两座水池，一座是月沼（牛胃），另外一座是南湖（牛肚）。月沼也称为北湖，始建于北宋时期，当时作当地人的生活用水。因为月沼的水与地下

which reads, "Poetry and books are the articles for guilding the world, while filial piety and fraternal respect are the foundation for passing on family tradition." The other couplet reads, "Doing good deeds is good; Starting a business is hard; Preserving what has been achieved is harder; Knowing the difficulties is not difficult."

Hongcun Village

Located in Yixian County, Huangshan City, Hongcun Village is famous for its unique Anhui architecture and beautiful natural scenery, known as the village in painting.

Hongcun Village is like a reclining brown cow by a river at the foot of a hill, and the cow-shaped village preserves intact groups of ancient buildings from the Ming and Qing dynasties, with Chengqi Tower and the rural dwellings on Woniu Mountain being particularly famous. Chengqi Tower was built during the Ming Dynasty and has a history of over 400 years. It is one of the oldest buildings in Hongcun Village and is known for its typical Huizhou-style of high wall, grand courtyard, horse head upturned corners, and white walls and black tiles. The Woniu Mountain dwellings are ancient dwellings from the Qing Dynasty, with exquisite decorative techniques such as wood carving and stone carving.

There are two ponds in Hongcun Village: one is Moon Marsh (the cow stomach), and the other is South Lake (the cow belly). The Moon Marsh, also known as North Lake, which was built in the Northern Song Dynasty. It was originally built for the local people's water supply.

迎客天下
YING KE TIAN XIA

宏村月沼（樊成柱　摄）
The Moon Marsh in Hongcun Village (Photo by Fan Chengzhu)

水是连通的，于是有了明暗相间的河流，九曲十弯穿越家家户户就像牛肠。月沼池的周围是古色古香的徽州老房屋，在清澈的水中形成了梦幻般的美景。南湖建于月沼之后，横跨南湖上的步行石桥，最早可追溯到清末时期。当时为了南湖书院两岸往来便利，临时建起了一座木质的小栈道，后因损毁改建为石桥。有位国画大师看到这座桥很美，就像国画中的桥，所以就称之为"画桥"。静如处子的南湖与徽派建筑完美融合，将大自然

Because the water in the Moon Marsh is connected to the underground water, there are rivers with alternating light and dark sections and winding through the households like cow intestines. Surrounding the Moon Marsh are ancient Huizhou houses, creating a dreamlike scenery in the clear water. The pedestrian stone bridge spanning South Lake, built after the Moon Marsh, can be traced back to the late Qing Dynasty. At that time, a wooden boardwalk was temporarily built for the convenience of communication between the two sides of South Lake Academy. Later, it was rebuilt as a stone bridge due to damage. A Chinese painting master saw that this bridge was very beautiful, just like what is depicted in the traditional Chinese painting, so he called it "the painted bridge". The serene South Lake blends perfectly with Huizhou architecture, blending nature with cultural history, truly embodying the countryside that has emerged from traditional Chinese painting.

Ancient Huizhou Cultural Tourism Area

Ancient Huizhou Cultural Tourism Area is a national 5A-level scenic spot created by the five scenic spots in Shexian County and Huizhou District, which are relatively concentrated. It includes the Huizhou Ancient City, memorial archway group · Baojia Garden, Qiankou folk houses, Chengkan Village, and Tangmo Village, and gathers traditional cultural elements of Huizhou, such as ancient

迎客天下
YING KE TIAN XIA

徽州古城（樊成柱　摄）

The Huizhou Ancient City (Photo by Fan Chengzhu)

与人文历史相融合，不愧是国画里走出来的乡村。

古徽州文化旅游区

　　古徽州文化旅游区是由歙县、徽州区境内比较集中的五大景区"抱团"创建的国家 5A 级景区，包含了徽州古城、牌坊群·鲍家花园、潜口民宅、呈坎、唐模，聚集了古城生活、宗祠、牌坊、徽商、村落、民居等徽州传统文化元素，是徽文化完美鲜活的呈现。

city life, ancestral temple, memorial archway, Huizhou merchants, villages, and folk houses. It is a perfect and vivid presentation of Huizhou culture.

Huizhou Ancient City is known as a national historical and cultural city, and is one of the four well preserved ancient cities in China. Founded in the Qin Dynasty, since the Tang Dynasty, it has been the capital of Huizhou county, state, and prefecture, known as the birthplace of Huizhou Studies. Because the county government and the prefectural government are located in the same city, a unique style of "city within a city" has been formed. Huizhou Ancient City is divided into an inner city and an outer city, with four gates in the east, west, north, and south. In addition, there are also ancient streets and alleys. The scenic spots within the city include Huizhou Garden, Fish Dam, Xuguo Stone Archway, Doushan Street, Tao Xingzhi Memorial Hall, Xin'an Stele Garden, and Taibai Tower. The Fish Dam is located in Huicheng Town, Shexian County, Huangshan City. It was built in the Tang Dynasty and rebuilt in the Ming Dynasty, dating back nearly 1,400 years, and is one of China's famous ancient water conservancy projects, known as "the First Dujiangyan Irrigation Project in Jiangnan". The dam is made of many granite blocks weighing one or two tons, and the interlocking stone blocks can be clearly seen among them, which can reflect the exquisite skills and wisdom of Huizhou people. The Fish Dam was a place where Huizhou merchants set sail during the Ming and Qing dynasties to inherit the prosperity

迎客天下
YING KE TIAN XIA

徽州古城被誉为国家历史文化名城，是中国保存完好的四大古城之一。始建于秦朝，自唐代以来，一直是徽郡、州、府治所在地，被誉为徽学发祥地。由于县治与府治同在一座城内，于是形成了城套城的独特风格。徽州古城分内城、外廓，有东西南北4个门，此外还保留着古街、古巷等。城内景区包含徽园、渔梁坝、许国石坊、斗山街、陶行知纪念馆、新安碑园、太白楼等7处。渔梁坝位于黄山市歙县徽城镇渔梁村，始建于唐代，明代重建，距今近1400年，是中国古代著名的水利工程之一，被称为"江南第一都江堰"。大坝由许多重达一两吨的花岗岩砌成，石块之间能明显看到石锁相扣，可以感受到徽州人的精湛技艺和智慧。渔梁坝是明清时期徽商从这里启航承接家族兴旺的地方，历朝历代都把渔梁坝之兴衰作为徽州兴衰的标志。渔梁坝是几百年来新安江上大小商贾船队往来的一个重要码头，是名副其实的徽商之源。

牌坊群·鲍家花园由牌坊群和鲍家花园两个景区组成。牌坊群为明清时期古徽州建筑艺术的代表作，棠樾的七连座牌坊群不仅体现了徽文化程朱理学忠、孝、节、义伦理道德的概貌，也包括了内涵极为丰富的"以人为本"的人文历史，同时也是徽商纵横商界三百余年的重要见证。棠樾的七连座牌坊群包括鲍灿孝行坊、慈孝里坊、鲍文龄妻汪氏节孝坊、乐善好施

of their families. The rise and fall of the Fish Dam pier has been regarded as a symbol of the rise and fall of Huizhou throughout the dynasties. For hundreds of years, it has been an important dock for large and small merchant fleets on the Xin'an River, and is truly the source of Huizhou merchants.

The memorial archway group · Baojia Garden consists of the memorial archway group and the Baojia Garden. The memorial archway group is a representative example of ancient Huizhou architecture in the Ming and Qing dynasties. The seven-archway group in Tangyue not only reflects the general outlook of Cheng-Zhu Neo Confucianism ethical principles of "loyalty, filial piety, chastity, and righteousness" in Huizhou culture, but also includes a rich and diverse human history with a focus on "people-centeredness". It is also an important witness to the Huizhou merchants' thriving in the business world for over 300 years. The seven-archway group in Tangyue includes the filial piety archway of Bao Can, the filial piety archway of Ci Xiaoli, the filial piety archway of Bao Wenling's wife Wang Shi, the charity archway, the filial piety archway of Bao Wenyan's second wife Wu Shi, the filial son archway of Bao Fengchang, and the prime minister archway of Bao Xiangxian, each of which has a touching story. The Baojia Garden is renowned as "the Mother of Eastern Gardens" and was originally the private garden of the famous Anhui businessman and Salt Tax Inspector, Bao Qiyun, during the Qianlong and Jiaqing years of the Qing Dynasty. It is a fine example of a traditional

棠樾牌坊群（樊成柱　摄）

Tangyue memorial archway group (Photo by Fan Chengzhu)

坊、鲍文渊继妻吴氏节孝坊、鲍逢昌孝子坊、鲍象贤尚书坊等，每一座牌坊都有一个动人故事。鲍家花园有着"东方园林之母"的美誉，原为清乾隆、嘉庆年间著名徽商、盐法道员鲍启运的私家花园，是典型的古徽派园林与徽派盆景相结合的中国私家园林精品。清末太平天国战争时遭到毁坏，现经修复重建，成为我国最大的私家园林和盆景观赏地。

潜口民宅是一座古建筑专题博物馆，位于黄山市徽州区潜口镇紫霞山麓，由明园和清园两部分组成，分别于1990年和2007年建成并对外开放。按照"原拆原建、集中保护"的原则，集中保护了明清时期最典型的古民居、古祠堂、古牌坊、古亭、古桥、古戏台等24幢古建筑，是研究中国古建筑学的珍贵实例，被誉为"我国明代民间艺术的活专著""人文景观和自然景观高度和谐统一的典范"。著名古建筑专家、故宫博物院前副院长单士元先生曾叹之曰："观皇宫去北京，

ancient Huizhou-style garden combined with Huizhou-style potted landscapes, and is among the finest private gardens in China. It was destroyed during the Taiping Heavenly Kingdom Movement in the late Qing Dynasty, but has now been restored and rebuilt to become China's largest private garden and a major potted landscape appreciation site.

Qiankou residential houses is a museum of ancient architecture, located at the foot of Zixia Mountain, Qiankou Town, Huizhou District, Huangshan City. It consists of Ming Garden and Qing Garden, which were completed and opened to the public in 1990 and 2007 respectively. In accordance with the principle of "original demolition and centralized protection", 24 ancient buildings, including the most typical ancient dwellings, ancient ancestral temples, ancient memorial archways, ancient pavilions, ancient bridges, and ancient theaters in the Ming and Qing dynasties, have been intensively protected. It is a precious example of studying Chinese ancient architecture, and is known as "a living monograph of folk art in the Ming Dynasty in China" and "a model of highly harmonious and unified human landscape and natural landscape". Shan Shiyuan, a renowned expert in ancient architecture and former deputy director of the Palace Museum, once said, "Visit the imperial palace in Beijing, and see the folk houses in Qiankou."

Chengkan, originally named Longxi, was built during the Eastern Han and Three Kingdoms periods. As early as the Song Dynasty, it was praised by the famous philosopher

潜口民宅（樊成柱　摄）

Qiankou residential house (Photo by Fan Chengzhu)

看民宅到潜口。"

　　呈坎原名龙溪，始建于东汉三国时期，早在宋朝就被著名理学家朱熹赞誉为"江南第一村"。现拥有国家级重点保护文物21处，被誉为"国宝之乡"。古老的九巷宛如迷宫，龙溪河宛如玉带，村落周边矗立着

Zhu Xi—"the first village in Jiangnan". There are currently 21 national key protected cultural relics, known as "the hometown of national treasures". The ancient nine alleys are like a maze, the Longxi River is like a jade belt, and eight mountains stand around the village, naturally forming the eight directions of the Eight Trigrams, together forming the

呈坎（樊成柱　摄）

Chengkan (Photo by Fan Chengzhu)

八座大山，自然形成了八卦的八个方位，共同构成了天然八卦布局。呈坎是全国保存最为完好的古村落之一，完整保存着宋、元、明等朝代以来的古建筑群体，汇集了徽派不同风格的亭、台、楼、阁、桥、井、祠、

natural layout of the Eight Trigrams. Chengkan is one of the best-preserved ancient villages in China, complete with a group of ancient buildings from the Song, Yuan, Ming and other dynasties, and featuring a variety of pavilions, towers, buildings, bridges, wells, ancestral halls, temples, and

迎客天下
YING KE TIAN XIA

社及民居，精湛的工艺及巧夺天工的石雕、砖雕、木雕，把古、大、美、雅的徽派建筑艺术体现得淋漓尽致。中国国画大师刘海粟曾说过"登黄山不可不去呈坎"。这里千百年来传承着"游呈坎一生无坎"的传奇过坎文化。

山水秀美是黄山最靓丽的颜值，文化灿烂是黄山最具国际标识度的价值，黄山市立足于得天独厚的自然山水、博大精深的徽州文化，坚持以文塑旅、以旅彰文，深入推进文旅融合，打通黄山走向世界的文旅条形码，黄山正在徐徐展开大黄山世界级休闲度假康养旅游目的地的宏伟蓝图。

residential buildings in the Huizhou-style architecture. The exquisite craftsmanship, and skilled stone and brick carvings, and wood carvings showcase the elegant and beautiful Huizhou-style architectural art to perfection. Chinese traditional painting master Liu Haisu once said, "It is a must to visit Chengkan when climbing Mount Huangshan." The legendary culture of overcoming obstacles has been passed down for thousands of years with the slogan "Traveling to Chengkan means a life without obstacles."

The beautiful scenery of mountains and waters is the most attractive aspect of Huangshan, and the brilliant culture is the most internationally identifiable value of Huangshan. Huangshan City, based on the unique natural landscape and profound Huizhou culture, insists on using culture to shape tourism and using tourism to highlight culture, and deepens the integration of culture and tourism. This will enable Huangshan to establish a cultural and tourism code that connects it to the world. Huangshan is slowly launching the grand blueprint of the Grant Huangshan world-class leisure and healthcare tourism destination.

人文徽州
底蕴深厚

郭沫若先生曾说："全国文物之最在安徽，安徽文物之最在徽州。徽州是文物之海。"徽州文化博大精深、璀璨夺目，徽商、徽州建筑、徽派篆刻、徽派版画、新安医学、徽州工艺及徽菜等在岁月的长河中，犹如一颗颗璀璨明珠，诠释着徽州文化的辉煌与鼎盛、智慧与魅力、匠心与美丽。

3

Humanistic Huizhou with Rich and Profound Heritage

Guo Moruo once said, "The most precious cultural relics in the country are in Anhui, and the most precious cultural relics in Anhui are in Huizhou. Huizhou is a sea of cultural relics." Huizhou culture is extensive and profound, resplendent and dazzling. In the long river of time, Huizhou merchants, Huizhou architecture, Huizhou seal cutting, Huizhou woodblock prints, Xin'an medicine, Huizhou handicrafts, and Huizhou cuisine and so on, like the brilliant pearls, interpreting the glory and prosperity, wisdom and charm, ingenuity and beauty of the Huizhou culture.

迎客天下
YING KE TIAN XIA

来到徽州，看得见的地表明珠当属徽派建筑，看不见的、流淌在徽州人血液中的匠心传承当属非物质文化遗产。

徽州名人辈出，据有关学者统计，有文献可证而为之立传者多达5399人。他们各怀经纶、各擅专长、各执技艺，广泛涉及政治、经济、军事、哲学等各个领域，为徽州文化贡献了璀璨的成果，如王茂荫是《资本论》里提到的唯一的中国人。

徽派建筑　　水墨画卷

受徽州文化传统和地理位置等因素的影响，徽州形成独具一格的徽派建筑风格。粉墙、青瓦、马头墙、砖木石雕以及层楼叠院、高脊飞檐、曲径回廊、亭台楼榭等的和谐组合，构成徽派建筑的重要元素。

建筑结构

马头墙

徽州人喜欢聚族而居，民居建筑密度很大。一家挨着一家，一户挨着一户，左勾右连。万一哪户失火了，难免会殃及池鱼。为了防患于未然，家家在屋顶上垒起了高高的马头墙，故而马头墙又被称为封火墙。同时，这个坚固的屏障也可防盗、防雷。马头墙的尖头部位与现代建筑中避雷针原理相似，无论怎样电闪

When coming to Huizhou, the visible surface pearl is the Huizhou architecture. The intangible craftsmanship inheritance flowing in the blood of the Huizhou people is the intangible cultural heritage.

Huizhou has brought forth numerous famous people. According to statistics by relevant scholars, there are as many as 5,399 people with documented records for whom biographies have been written. They each possess outstanding abilities, specialize in different fields, and master various skills, widely involving various fields such as politics, economy, military, and philosophy. They have contributed brilliant achievements to Huizhou culture. For example, Wang Maoyin is the only Chinese mentioned in *Capital*.

Huizhou-Style Architecture in Ink and Wash Paintings

Influenced by factors such as Huizhou cultural traditions and geographical location, Huizhou has formed a unique Huizhou-style architecture. The harmonious combination of white walls, black tiles, horse-head walls, brick-wood-stone carvings, as well as multi-storey courtyards, high ridged and upturned eaves, winding paths and corridors, pavilions and terraces, constitutes important elements of Huizhou-style architecture.

马头墙（邱黎　摄）

The horse-head walls (Photo by Qiu Li)

雷鸣，马头墙都会挺身而出，哪怕是墙毁瓦裂，也会保证主体建筑完好无损。至于防风防雨的作用，就更显而易见了。除了保护建筑的功用，马头墙也承担着一定的文化功能。马头墙墙肩的做法多种多样，其退阶尺寸会随山墙高矮以及出檐大小而灵活变动。马头墙有一阶、二阶、三阶、四阶之分，也可称为一叠式、两叠式、三叠式、四叠式。阶数越多，意味着这个家庭历史越久，地位更高，最多的可至五叠。

门楼

徽派建筑大门，均配有门楼（规模稍小的称为门罩），主要作用是防止雨水顺墙而下溅到门上。门楼

Architectural Structure
The Horse-Head Walls

Huizhou people like to live together in clans, and the density of residential buildings is very high. House by house and household by household are closely connected. If one of the houses caught fire, it was inevitable that others would be affected as well. To prevent disasters before they occur, every family built high horse-head walls on the roofs. Therefore, the horse-head walls are also called fire-sealing walls. At the same time, this solid barrier can also prevent theft and lightning. The pointed parts of the horse-head walls are similar to the principle of lightning rods in modern buildings. No matter how thunder and lightning strike, the horse-head walls will step forward. Even if the walls are damaged and the tiles are broken, the main building will remain intact. As for the functions of preventing wind and rain, they are even more obvious. In addition to protecting the building, the horse-head walls also undertake certain cultural functions. There are various ways of making the wall shoulders of the horse-head walls, and the step-back dimensions will change flexibly according to the height of the gable walls and the size of the eaves overhanging. The horse-head walls are divided into one step, two steps, three steps, and four steps, which can also be called one-fold, two-fold, three-fold, and four-fold. The more steps there are, the longer the family's history is and the higher its status is. The most one can reach five folds.

迎客天下
YING KE TIAN XIA

是住宅的脸面，是体现主人地位的标志。一般农家的门罩较为简单，在离门框上部少许的位置，用水磨砖砌出向外挑的檐脚，顶上覆瓦，并刻一些简单的装饰。富家门楼十分讲究，多有砖雕或石雕装潢。徽州区岩寺镇进士第门楼三间四柱五楼，仿明代牌坊而建，用青石和水磨砖混合建成，门楼横枋上双狮戏球雕饰，形象生动，刀工细腻，柱两侧配有巨大的抱鼓石，高雅华贵。徽派建筑门楼上砖雕题材丰富，有着较强的民俗色彩，隐喻性、象征性强，如安徽博物院藏清《百子图》，为徽派砖雕的代表作，画面层次所雕百个顽童形态各异，神韵毕现，栩栩如生，象征多子多福。

高墙深宅

徽州有许多古民居，四周均用高墙围起，远望似一座座古堡，房屋除大门外，只开少数小窗，采光主要靠天井。这种居宅往往很深，进门为前庭，中设天井，后设厅堂，一般住人。厅堂后用中门隔开，设一堂二卧室。堂室后又是一道高墙，靠墙设天井，两旁建厢房。这是第一进。第二进的结构为一脊分两堂，前后两天井，中有隔扇，有卧室四间，堂室两个。第三进、第四进或者往后的更多进，结构大抵相同。这种深宅里居住的都是一个家族。随着子孙的繁衍，房子也就一进一进地套建起来，故房子大者有"三十六天井，七十二槛窗"之说。一般是一个支系住一进。

Gate Towers

The gates of Huizhou-style architecture are all equipped with gate towers (those on a slightly smaller scale are called door hoods). The main function is to prevent rainwater from splashing onto the doors along the walls. The gate tower is the face of the residence and a sign reflecting the status of the owner. The door hoods of ordinary farmers' houses are relatively simple. At a position a little above the door frame, the eave's feet that jut out are built with terrazzo bricks, covered with tiles on the top, and some simple decorations are carved. The gate towers of wealthy families are very particular and mostly decorated with brick or stone carvings. The gate tower of the Jinshi Residence in Yansi Town, Huizhou District, has three bays, four columns, and five floors. It is built imitating the memorial archway of the Ming Dynasty and is made of a mixture of bluestone and terrazzo bricks. The double lions playing with a ball carved on the horizontal beam of the gate tower are vivid, and the carving work is exquisite. There are huge drum-shaped stones on both sides of the columns, which are elegant and luxurious. The brick carvings on the gate towers of Huizhou-style architecture have rich themes and many folk elements, with metaphorical and symbolic meanings. For example, the *Picture of One Hundred Children* of the Qing Dynasty collected in the Anhui Museum is a representative work of Huizhou-style brick carvings. One hundred naughty children carved in different postures on the picture's layers are vivid

徽州的高墙深宅（邱黎　摄）

The houses with high walls in Huizhou (Photo by Qiu Li)

门一闭，各家各户独立过日子；门一开，一个大门出入，一个祖宗牌下祭祀。它生动地体现了古徽州聚族而居的民风。这种高墙深宅的建筑，以及千丁之族未尝散居的民风，在国内是罕见的。

and lifelike, with all their charm shown, symbolizing having many children and much happiness.

High Walls and Deep Courtyards

There are many ancient dwellings in Huizhou. They are all surrounded by high walls. From a distance, they look like castles. Apart from the main gate, only a few small windows are opened. The main source of lighting is the patios. Such residences are often very deep. Entering the door is the front courtyard, with a patio in the middle and a hall at the back, where people usually live. The hall is separated by a central door at the back, with one hall and two bedrooms. Behind the hall is another high wall. Against the wall is a patio, with wing rooms on both sides. This is the first entrance. The structure of the second entrance is one roof dividing into two halls, with two patios at the front and back. There are partition boards in the middle, four bedrooms, and two halls. The third entrance, the fourth entrance, or more entrances further back are generally similar in structure. A whole family lives in such a deep residence. As the descendants multiply, the houses are built one entrance after another. Therefore, for large houses, there is a saying of "thirty-six patios and seventy-two sash windows". Generally, one branch of the family lives in one entrance. With the doors closed, each household lives an independent life; with the doors opened, people enter and exit through one main gate and offer sacrifices under one ancestral tablet. It vividly reflects the folk custom of Huizhou people

迎客天下
YING KE TIAN XIA

徽派"三雕"

徽派"三雕"指具有徽派风格的砖雕、石雕、木雕三种中国民间雕刻工艺,主要用于民居、祠堂、庙宇、园林等建筑的装饰,以及古式家具、笔筒、果盘等工艺雕刻。

砖雕

前文中已提到,砖雕广泛用于徽派风格的门楼、门套、门楣、屋檐、屋顶、屋瓴等处,使建筑物显得典雅、庄重,是徽派建筑艺术的重要组成部分。砖雕有平雕、浮雕、立体雕刻,题材包括翎毛花卉、龙虎狮象、林园山水、戏剧人物等,具有浓郁的民间色彩。徽州砖雕的用料与制作考究。一般采用经特殊技艺烧

砖雕(黄跃明 摄)
The brick carving (Photo by Huang Yueming)

living together in clans in ancient times. The architecture of such high walls and deep courtyards, and the folk custom that a clan of thousands of people never live scattered are rare in the country.

Three Kinds of Huizhou-Style Carvings

Three kinds of Huizhou-style carvings refer to three Chinese folk carving techniques of brick carving, stone carving, and wood carving with Huizhou style. They are mainly used for the decorations of buildings such as residential houses, ancestral halls, temples, and gardens, as well as the craft carvings of antique furniture, pen holders, and fruit plates.

Brick Carving

As mentioned above, brick carving is widely used in gate towers, door pockets, lintels, eaves, roofs, and ridges of Huizhou-style buildings, making the buildings elegant and solemn. It is an important part of Huizhou-style architectural art. Brick carving includes flat carvings, relief carvings, and three-dimensional carvings. The themes include feathers, flowers, dragons, tigers, lions, elephants, gardens, mountains, waters, drama characters, etc., with many folk elements. The materials and production of Huizhou brick carving are exquisite. Generally, blue bricks that are fired with special techniques, make a clear sound when dropped, have pure color, and are used as materials. First, they are finely ground into blanks, the parts of the picture are outlined on them, the depths of the objects are carved out, and the distance and

迎客天下
YING KE TIAN XIA

制、掷地有声、色泽纯清的青砖为材料,先细磨成坯,在上面勾勒出画面的部位,凿出物象的深浅,确定画面的远近层次,然后再根据各个部位的轮廓进行精心刻画,局部"出细",使事先设计好的图案一一凸显出来。砖雕在徽州诸地随处可见。古老民居、祠堂、庙宇等建筑物上镶嵌的砖雕,虽经岁月的磨砺,风雨的剥蚀,依然玲珑剔透,耐人寻味。

石雕

石雕是徽派建筑精美细节的完美体现,主要用于各种徽派建筑的装饰,享誉甚高。它主要取材于青黑色的黟县青和褐色的茶园石。黟县青又名"黟县清水石",被民间称为世界两大"活石"之一。黟县山上

石雕(邱黎 摄)

The stone carving (Photo by Qiu Li)

hierarchy of the picture are determined. Then, careful carving is carried out according to the outlines of each part, and the details are refined locally, so that the pre-designed patterns emerge one by one. Brick carving can be seen everywhere in Huizhou. The brick carving embedded in ancient residential houses, ancestral halls, temples and other buildings is still exquisite and thought-provoking despite the grinding of years and the erosion of wind and rain.

Stone Carving

Stone carving is the perfect manifestation of the exquisite details of Huizhou-style architecture and is mainly used for the decoration of various Huizhou-style architecture, enjoying a very high reputation. It is mainly sourced from the blue-black Yixian Green and the brown Tea Garden Stone. Yixian Green is also known as "Yixian Qingshui Stone" and is called one of the two "living stones" in the world. There are many bluestones produced in the mountains of Yixian County, that is, the Yixian Green marble. This kind of bluestone is located in the high mountains and has been bathed in clouds and fog. The stone is moderately hard and soft, and has always been mostly used for building and stone carving. The themes of stone carving are restricted by the carving materials and are not as complex as wood carving and brick carving. They are mainly images of animals and plants, archaize patterns and calligraphy, while character stories and landscapes are relatively rare. But the knife techniques are exquisite and generous, and the styles are mainly shallow relief carving,

迎客天下
YING KE TIAN XIA

多产青石,即"黟县青"大理石。这种青石处于高山,饱经云雾沐浴,石质软硬适度,历来多用于建材和石雕。石雕题材受雕刻资料自身限制,不及木雕与砖雕复杂,主要是动植物形象、博古纹样和书法,至于人物故事与山水则较为少见,但刀法精致大方,风格以浅层透雕、平雕和圆雕为主。圆雕整合趋势明显,刀法精致且质朴大方。在刀与石碰撞出的艺术中,石雕已成为凝固徽州文化的唯美符号。底蕴深厚、沉稳奔放、姿态各异而不逾矩的徽州石雕作品,象征着徽州人处事不轻不重,内敛而不张扬的性格。

木雕

木雕也是主要用于徽派建筑上的装饰。在徽派宅院内的屏风、窗楣、栏柱上均可一睹木雕的风采,几乎是无村不有。徽派建筑中木雕的题材广泛,有人物、山水、花卉、禽兽、虫鱼、云头、回纹、八宝博古、文字锡联及各种吉祥图案等。根据徽派建筑物体的部件需要与可能,采用圆雕、浮雕、透雕等表现手法。明代初年,徽派建筑中的木雕已初具规模,雕风拙朴粗犷,以平面淡浮雕手法为主。明中叶以后,随着徽商财力的增强,炫耀乡里的意识日益浓厚,木雕艺术也逐渐向精雕细刻过渡,多层透雕取代平面浅雕成为主流。徽派建筑中木雕的代表是黟县卢村的木雕楼,它体现了徽派民居的精华。卢村木雕楼是由七家里民

flat carving and round carving. The round carving shows an obvious integration trend, and the knife techniques combine exquisiteness with simplicity and generosity. In the art created by the collision of the knife and the stone, stone carving has become an aesthetic symbol that solidifies Huizhou culture. With profound connotations, calm and unrestrained, and presenting different postures without overstepping the rules, Huizhou stone carving works symbolize the character of Huizhou people who handle affairs neither too lightly nor too heavily, being reserved and not ostentatious.

Wood Carving

Wood carving is also mainly used for the decoration of Huizhou architecture. The charm of wood carving can be seen on the screens, window lattices, and column balustrades in Huizhou-style courtyards, and it almost exists in every village. The themes of the wood carving are extensive, including figures, landscapes, flowers, birds, animals, insects, fish, cloud patterns, fret patterns, archaize patterns with eight precious things, couplets inlaid with metal characters, and various auspicious patterns, etc. Wood carving adopts expression techniques such as round carving, relief carving, and openwork carving according to the needs and possibilities of the components of Huizhou-style architecture. In the early years of the Ming Dynasty, the wood carving in Huizhou-style architecture had begun to take shape, with a simple and rough carving style, mainly using the flat bas-relief technique. After the middle of the Ming Dynasty, with

迎客天下
YING KE TIAN XIA

木雕（黄跃明　摄）

The wood carving (Photo by Huang Yueming)

居组成的木雕楼群，主要包括志诚堂、思济堂、思成堂、玻璃厅等宅院。

徽派建筑壁画

徽派建筑壁画是壁画的一种。壁画，就是绘在壁面上的画，是人类历史上最早的绘画形式之一。壁画有岩画、洞窟壁画、宫廷壁画、墓室壁画、寺观壁画和民居壁画等多个种类。徽州壁画属于民居壁画。徽州建筑壁画有记载古徽州当地风土人情和徽派建筑历史的"活化石"之美称，受到众多从事徽学研究的考古学家、民俗学家的重视。

徽州建筑壁画以美刻骨，以意铸魂。

the increase of the financial power of Huizhou merchants and the growing consciousness of showing off in the hometown, the wood carving art gradually transitioned to elaborate carving, and multi-layer openwork carving replaced flat shallow carving to become the mainstream. The representative of wood carving in Huizhou-style architecture is the Wood Carving Building in Lucun Village, Yixian County, which reflects the essence of Huizhou-style dwellings. The Wood Carving Building is a group of wood carving buildings composed of dwellings of seven families, mainly including Zhicheng Hall, Siji Hall, Sicheng Hall, Glass Hall and other courtyards.

Huizhou-Style Architectural Murals

The Huizhou-style architectural murals are one type of murals. Murals are paintings that are painted on walls and are one of the earliest forms of painting in human history. There are many types of murals, including rock paintings, cave paintings, palace murals, tomb chamber murals, temple and shrine murals, and residential murals. Huizhou-style architectural murals belong to residential murals. The Huizhou-style architectural murals are known as "living fossils" that record the local customs and history of ancient Huizhou and are highly valued by archaeologists and folklorists engaged in Huizhou studies.

The Huizhou-style architectural murals are not only aesthetically captivating but also deeply imbued with meaning.

The folk painters of Huizhou-style architectural murals

迎客天下
YING KE TIAN XIA

徽派建筑壁画《徽州童子图》（胡晓耕 摄）

Huizhou-style architectural mural *Young Kids of Huizhou* (Photo by Hu Xiaogeng)

　　徽州建筑壁画民间画师使用自制的植物、矿物颜料填彩，色彩以朱砂、赭石、藤黄、靛蓝、石绿和黑色为主。绘画形式也很有特色，人物、花鸟以工笔为主，山水景物以写意为主，多用以工代写的手法来体现壁画创作的主题风格。徽州建筑壁画，宿在民居，停于楼阁，绕在庭院，傍着屋梁，清清淡淡、以美刻骨、独具魅力。

　　徽州建筑壁画是一种平易近人的民间艺术，浸润着时光与民俗的浓重烟火气，内容十分丰富，意蕴十分深邃。有体现"仁、义、礼、智"和"忠、廉、耻、

used homemade plant and mineral pigments, with the main colors—vermilion, ochre, gamboge, indigo, emerald green, and black. The painting style is also very distinctive, with figures, flowers and birds mainly depicted in "fine brushwork" and landscapes mainly in "free brushwork". The technique of "using fine brushwork to replace writing" is often used to convey the themes and styles of the mural creations. The Huizhou-style architectural murals are found in the dwellings, lodged in the pavilions, winding around the courtyards, nestling by the beams, with a delicate and elegant beauty that is uniquely captivating.

Huizhou-style architectural murals are a down-to-earth folk art that is imbued with the heavy aroma of time and folk customs. Their content is very rich and their connotation is profound. There are character paintings that embody Confucian virtues, such as benevolence, righteousness, propriety, wisdom, loyalty, integrity, shame, courage, sincerity, and reverence, for example *King Wen of Zhou Visits the Sage* and *Sanniang Teaches Her Sons*. There are flower and bird paintings and paintings of people, such as *Young Kids of Huizhou*, which depict auspicious wealth. There are also bamboo and stone paintings that emphasize the spirit and integrity, and landscape paintings that emphasize the harmony between man and nature. In general, the Huizhou-style architectural murals mostly reflect the good wishes of the common people to ward off evil spirits, celebrate happiness, and promote moral education.

迎客天下
YING KE TIAN XIA

勇、诚、敬"等儒家思想的人物画，如《文王访贤》《三娘教子》等；也有以喜庆富贵为内容的花鸟、人物画，如《徽州童子图》；还有以气、节为重的竹石画和以天人合一为主题的山水画。总的来说，徽州建筑壁画大多反映了百姓驱邪纳祥、喜庆欢愉、道德教化的良好愿望。

虽然徽州彩绘壁画在清末、民国之后，随着徽商的衰败而濒危，但依然留下了一批画师在古民居维修和传统徽派民居建设中发挥作用，为徽州的后代子民留下了瑰丽无比的文化遗产和精神风标。

匠心文化　非遗传承

非物质文化遗产是徽州文化传承积淀中最具魅力的文化符号之一，是最为亮丽的文化名片之一。黄山作为徽州文化的重要发祥地，拥有大量的徽州非物质文化资源，同时也有很多的优秀传承人。

截至 2023 年底，徽州文化生

徽派建筑壁画《三娘教子》（胡晓耕 摄）
Huizhou-style architectural mural *Sanniang Teaches Her Sons* (Photo by Hu Xiaogeng)

Although Huizhou-style architectural murals were in danger of disappearing after the decline of the Huizhou merchants in the late Qing Dynasty and early Republic of China, a group of painters still played a role in repairing ancient residential buildings and constructing some traditional Huizhou-style residences, leaving a magnificent cultural heritage and spiritual landmark for the descendants of the ancient Huizhou people.

Ingenious Culture, Inheritance of Intangible Cultural Heritage

Intangible cultural heritage is one of the most charming cultural symbol and one of the most beautiful cultural calling card in the accumulation of Huizhou culture inheritance. As an important birthplace of Huizhou culture, Huangshan has a large number of Huizhou intangible cultural resources and also many excellent inheritors.

By the end of 2023, the Huizhou Cultural Ecology Reserve has 5 items in the UNESCO *Representative List of the Intangible Cultural Heritage of Humanity*, 24 national-level representative intangible cultural heritages, 78 provincial-level items, 148 municipal-level items, and 317 district/county-level items; 33 national-level representative inheritors of intangible cultural heritage, 201 provincial-level inheritors, 750 municipal-level inheritors, and 794 district/county-level inheritors. It has 4 national-level

迎客天下
YING KE TIAN XIA

态保护区拥有列入联合国教科文组织《人类非物质文化遗产代表作名录》的非物质遗产5项,国家级非遗代表性项目24项、省级78项、市级148项、区县级317项;国家级非遗代表性传承人33人、省级201人、市级750人、区县级794人;拥有国家级非遗生产性保护示范基地4处、省级传承基地20处、省级非遗工坊3处、市级非遗传习基地122处。全市现存的非遗种类和数量在安徽省地市中均位列第一。让我们一起来走近徽州非遗,聆听当代非遗优秀传承人书写的传承故事!

国家级非遗"中医诊法"(张一帖内科疗法)传承人

中医,国之瑰宝。李济仁、张舜华夫妇是张一帖内科疗法国家级代表性传承人、新安名医张一帖第十四代传承人。

张舜华,幼随其父张根桂习医,习得祖传绝技,1950年开始悬壶济世,在乡间日夜出诊,张舜华以高超医术被誉为"女张一帖"。1958年,张舜华夫妇将祖传"十八罗汉"末药秘方毅然献给国家,受到安徽省卫生厅、《安徽日报》等高度重视和表彰。张舜华行医60余年,擅长内、妇科,以及对感病、急性热病,诊病特点在于认症准,用药猛,择药专,剂量重。

张舜华的先生李济仁是全国首批"国医大师"、首

demonstration bases for productive protection of intangible cultural heritage, 20 provincial-level inheritance bases, 3 provincial-level intangible cultural heritage workshops, and 122 municipal-level intangible cultural heritage inheritance and learning bases. The types and quantities of the existing intangible cultural heritages in the city rank first among the prefecture-level cities in Anhui Province. Let's approach the Huizhou intangible cultural heritages together and listen to the stories written by the outstanding contemporary inheritors of intangible cultural heritages!

The Inheritor of the National Intangible Cultural Heritage "Traditional Chinese Medicine Diagnostic Method" (Zhang Yitie's Internal Medicine Therapy)

Traditional Chinese medicine is a national treasure. Li Jiren and Zhang Shunhua, the couple, are the national-level representative inheritors of Zhang Yitie's internal medicine therapy and the 14th-generation inheritors of the famous doctor Zhang Yitie in Xin'an.

Zhang Shunhua learned medicine from her father Zhang Gengui when she was young and mastered the unique ancestral skills. In 1950, she began to practice medicine to help the people. She made house calls day and night in the countryside and was praised as the "female Zhang Yitie" for her superb medical skills. In 1958, the couple resolutely donated the secret recipe of the ancestral "Eighteen Arhats" myrrh to the country, which was highly valued and commended by the Anhui Provincial Health Department and *Anhui Daily*. Having

迎客天下
YING KE TIAN XIA

李济仁、张舜华夫妇（张雨涵 摄）

Li Jiren and Zhang Shunhua (Photo by Zhang Yuhan)

批"全国 500 名老中医"、国务院政府特殊津贴获得者、中华中医药学会终身成就奖获得者。

国家级非遗"歙砚制作技艺"传承人

歙砚，徽州文房四宝之一。郑寒是第三批国家级非物质文化遗产项目歙砚制作技艺代表性传承人。他于 1979 年踏上专业砚雕之路，2005 年创办黄山市郑寒砚雕艺术中心，擅长山水、人物、花鸟砚的制作，刀法遒劲、老辣、简练，雕刻上深、透、镂、点、线、面的结合极其完美。构思巧妙、擅用石色纹理是他的独到之处。作品师古不拘古，创作中崇尚来源于自然的法则，认为"外师造化，中得心源"。郑寒从事歙砚

practiced medicine for more than 60 years, she is good at internal medicine, gynecology, exogenous diseases and acute febrile diseases. The characteristics of her diagnosis lie in accurate identification, powerful medication, specialized drug selection, and heavy dosage.

Li Jiren, the husband of Zhang Shunhua, is one of the first batch of National Masters of Traditional Chinese Medicine in the country, one of the first batch of 500 Elderly Traditional Chinese Medicine Doctors in the Country, a recipient of the special government allowance of the State Council, and a recipient of the Lifetime Achievement Award of the China Association of Chinese Medicine.

The Inheritor of the National Intangible Cultural Heritage "She Inkstone Making Technique"

She Inkstone is one of the Four Treasures of the Study in Huizhou. Zheng Han is a representative inheritor of She Inkstone Making Technique of the third batch of the national intangible cultural heritage project. He embarked on the path of professional inkstone carving in 1979 and founded Zheng Han Inkstone Carving Art Center in Huangshan City in 2005. He is good at making inkstones with landscapes, figures, flowers, and birds. His knife techniques are powerful, seasoned, and concise. The combination of deep carving, transparency, openwork, dotting, lines, and surfaces in the carving is flawless. Clever conception and good use of the stone color and texture are his unique features. He learns from the ancients but is not bound by the ancients. In

迎客天下
YING KE TIAN XIA

的创作、挖掘、整理、保护、研究和开发达 30 多年，有着丰富的实践经验和艺术修养，在我国歙砚制作艺术界有很高声誉和影响。作品《黄山胜迹印痕砚》和《中国龙砚》分别被选作赠送日本明仁天皇和法国前总统希拉克的国礼，他被誉为"中国第一国礼砚雕家"。2008 年，《天圆地方罗盘砚》被市政府选作赠送国际奥委会终身名誉主席萨马兰奇的礼品。

歙砚传承人郑寒在创作（郑寒工作室　摄）
Zheng Han, the inheritor of She Inkstone, is creating an inkstone (Photo by Zheng Han Studio)

《中国龙砚》（郑寒　摄）
Chinese Dragon Inkstone (Photo by Zheng Han)

国家级非遗"徽墨制作技艺"传承人

徽墨，中国名墨之一。汪培坤是第三批安徽省非物质文化遗产徽墨制作技艺项目代表性传承人。他 16 岁拜师学艺，先师从徽州著名歙砚雕刻大师吴水清学习砚雕技艺，后师从徽墨著名制模大师胡成锦和胡开文、第七代徽墨传承人胡连生学习徽墨制作、墨模雕刻技艺。在几十年实践

creation, he advocates the laws from nature and believes that "External objects are the source of creation, and inspiration comes from the inner heart." Zheng Han has been engaged in the creation, excavation, collation, protection, research, and development of She Inkstone for more than 30 years. He has rich practical experience and artistic accomplishment and enjoys a high reputation and influence in the art circle of She Inkstone making in China. The works *Inkstone with Impressions of Huangshan's Scenic Spots* and *Chinese Dragon Inkstone* were selected as national gifts to be presented to Emperor Akihito of Japan and Jacques Chirac, the former president of France respectively, and he is hailed as the First National Gift Inkstone Carver in China. In 2008, the *Compass Inkstone with Round Sky and Square Earth* was selected by the municipal government as a gift to be presented to Juan Antonio Samaranch, the honorary life president of the International Olympic Committee.

The Inheritor of the National Intangible Cultural Heritage "Hui Ink Making Technique"

Hui Ink is one of the famous Chinese ink. Wang Peikun is a representative inheritor of the Hui Ink making technique project of the third batch of Anhui intangible cultural heritage. He began to learn from a master at the age of 16. First, he learned inkstone carving skills from Wu Shuiqing, a famous She Inkstone carving master in Huizhou. Later, he learned Hui Ink making and ink mold carving skills from Hu Chengjin and Hu kaiwen, famous Hui Ink mold masters,

迎客天下
YING KE TIAN XIA

中，他不仅摸索掌握了一套独具匠心的制墨工艺流程，并在徽墨理论和徽墨制作与墨模雕刻技艺上具备了很高的造诣。他努力传承、勇于开拓、因地取材，将徽州秀丽山水和悠久历史人文等作为主要素材，并将黄山四绝（奇松、云海、怪石、温泉）和徽州四雕（砖雕、木雕、石雕、竹雕）有机融入徽墨创作技艺中，使徽墨产品造型新颖雅致，内涵深刻隽永。他创新研发徽墨"幻彩法"描金技艺和失传已久的特制精细"漆烟墨"，具有质地细腻、香味浓郁、色泽黑润、经久不褪、舐纸不胶、入纸不晕的特点，目前在国内制墨业中绝无仅有。其代表作品有《六贤图》《宾虹宝墨》《徽州人家》《辋川图》等。

徽墨制作技艺传承人汪培坤（胡开文墨厂 摄）
Wang Peikun, the inheritor of Hui Ink making technology (Photo by Hu Kaiwen Ink Factory)

《宾虹宝墨》（胡开文墨厂 摄）
Binhong Ink Treasure (Photo by Hu Kaiwen Ink Factory)

and Hu Liansheng, the seventh-generation Hui Ink inheritor. During decades of practice, he not only explored and mastered a set of unique ink-making technological processes but also achieved superb attainments in Hui Ink theory, and Hui Ink making and ink mold carving skills. He makes efforts to inherit, dares to explore, and uses local materials. He takes the beautiful mountains and waters of Huizhou and the long history and culture as the main materials and organically integrates the Four Wonders of Mount Huangshan (Pines, sea of clouds, grotesque rocks, and hot spring) and the Four Carvings of Huizhou (brick, wood, stone, and bamboo) into the Hui Ink creation skills, making the Hui Ink products novel and elegant in shape with profound and meaningful connotations. He innovatively developed the "color-changing" gold tracing technique for Hui Ink and the long-lost special fine "lacquer soot ink", which has the characteristics of fine texture, rich fragrance, black and moist color, long-lasting colorfastness, no sticking to the paper when licked, and no halo when applied to the paper, which is unique in the current domestic ink-making industry. His representative works include *Six Sages Picture*, *Binhong Ink Treasure*, *Huizhou Families*, *Wangchuan Picture,* etc.

The Inheritor of the National Intangible Cultural Heritage "Huizhou Lacquerware Decorative Technique"

Huizhou lacquerware is one of the traditional handicrafts in Huizhou. It has a history of more than 1,000

迎客天下
YING KE TIAN XIA

国家级非遗"徽州漆器髹饰技艺"传承人

徽州漆器，徽州传统工艺品之一，具有1000多年的历史，徽州漆器中的螺钿漆在宋时被誉为"宋嵌"，而菠萝漆在南宋曾作为贡器。明清两代漆器工艺空前发展，争奇斗艳，蔚为大观。明代徽州漆工黄成所著《髹饰录》则是中国古代唯一流传的漆工专著。徽州漆器使用的主要原材料有生漆（植物漆）、桐油、木材、麻布、贝壳、各种天然色彩的玉石、金粉、金箔及牛骨、瓦灰、棉纸、猪血等。

甘而可在创作徽州漆器（罗培 摄）
Gan Erke is creating lacquerware (Photo by Luo Pei)

徽州漆器传承人肩负着这样的责任与理想：以文化为桥梁，让世界了解中国；以艺术为纽带，让中国走向世界。

甘而可，第三批国家级非物质文化遗产项目徽州漆器髹饰技艺代表性传承人。他师从老艺人汪福林、"楚漆国手"俞金海学习漆艺堆灰、木雕和砚雕，2012年，成立黄山市而可漆艺工作室，工作室一楼漆艺展

years. The mother-of-pearl lacquer in Huizhou lacquerware was praised as "Song Inlay" in the Song Dynasty, while the pineapple lacquer was used as tribute ware in the Southern Song Dynasty. During the Ming and Qing dynasties, the lacquerware craft achieved unprecedented development, competing with each other in beauty and presenting a magnificent sight. *Xiushi Lu* written by Huang Cheng, a Huizhou lacquerworker in the Ming Dynasty, is the only lacquerwork monograph handed down in ancient China. The main raw materials used in Huizhou lacquerware include raw lacquer (plant lacquer), tung oil, wood, linen, shells, jade stones in various natural colors, gold powder, gold foil, ox bones, tile ash, cotton paper, pig blood, etc.

The inheritors of Huizhou lacquerware bear such responsibilities and aspirations: Take culture as a bridge to let the world understand China; use art as a link to lead China to the world.

Gan Erke is a representative inheritor of the Huizhou Lacquerware Decorative Technique, in the third batch of the national intangible cultural heritage project. He learned the lacquer art of piled ashes, wood carving, and inkstone carving from the old artisans Wang Fulin, and Yu Jinhai, the master of Chu lacquer. In 2012, Erke Lacquer Art Studio in Huangshan City was established. The lacquer art exhibition hall on the first floor of the studio has been officially open to the public free all year round for better publicity of Huizhou lacquer art. Gan Erke can achieve the extreme in various mottled

迎客天下
YING KE TIAN XIA

厅常年对外免费开放和展示,以便更好地宣传徽州漆器艺术。甘而可对各类变涂髹饰技法能运用到极致,手工做出了机器的精度。其产品注重原创性,每件作品都具有新的创意。近年来,甘而可参加了多项国际交流活动,他的多件作品被故宫博物院、中国国家博物馆、大英博物馆、美国大都会艺术博物馆等世界知名博物馆收藏,精美的犀皮漆享誉海内外。其代表作品有《红金斑犀皮漆大圆盒》(被故宫博物院永久性收藏)、《绿金斑犀皮漆菱花盒》、《歙州漆砂砚》等。

《红金斑犀皮漆大圆盒》(李亮 摄)

Rhinoceros Leather Lacquer Box with Red and Gold Texture (Photo by Li Liang)

范福安,第四批安徽省非物质文化遗产项目徽州髹饰技艺代表性传承人,吉林艺术学院等多所高校研究生导师。他自幼受徽州传统文化浸染,对绘画有着异乎寻常的痴迷,师承俞金海等徽州漆器老艺人。因眷恋故土,2009年他回到屯溪,专心创作,并成立黄山市安海文化传播有限公司,从事漆器、漆画等艺术宣传、推广和传播。在继承新安传统漆画精髓的基础上,大胆创新,师法自然,醉心于漆艺创作,

lacquer decorative techniques and has achieved the precision of machines with his hands. His products focus on originality, making each work have new creative ideas. In recent years, Gan Erke has participated in a number of international exchange activities. Many of his works have been collected by world-renowned museums such as the palace Museum, the National Museum of China, the British Museum, and the Metropolitan Museum of Art. The exquisite rhinoceros hide lacquer is renowned at home and abroad. His representative works include *Rhinoceros Leather Lacquer Box with Red and Gold Texture* (permanently collected by the Palace Museum), *Rhinoceros Leather Lacquer Rhombus Box with Green and Gold Texture*, *Shezhou Lacquer Sand Inkstone*, etc.

Fan Fu'an is a representative inheritor of the Huizhou Decorative Technique, in the fourth batch of the intangible cultural heritage project of Anhui Province, and a postgraduate supervisor at multiple universities including Jilin University of Arts. Since childhood, influenced by Huizhou traditional culture, he has had an extraordinary obsession with painting and learned from old Huizhou lacquerware artisans such as Yu Jinhai, and so on. Due to his attachment to his hometown, he returned to Tunxi in 2009 to concentrate on creation and established Huangshan Anhai Cultural Communication Co., Ltd. to engage in the publicity, promotion, and dissemination of lacquerware, lacquer paintings and other arts. On the basis of inheriting the essence of the traditional Xin'an lacquer paintings, he boldly innovated, learned from nature,

迎客天下
YING KE TIAN XIA

范福安在进行漆画创作(范福安大漆艺术馆 摄)
Fan Fu'an is creating a lacquerware painting (Photo by Fan Fu'an Lacquerware Museum)

自成一派,不仅能够让人领略到当代艺术家清逸的文化气息和静谧高雅的艺术品位,还能够感受到传统文化的滋养和浸润。其代表作品《渔歌唱晚》获中国工艺美术精品博览会"国艺杯"金奖,《春雪》被中国工艺美术馆收藏,《少女的祈祷》入选第六届"JC雅各布森"肖像赛,在欧洲多国国家艺术博物馆巡展……诸多荣耀让他迈向世界的底气更足。走出去,世界就在眼前。为庆祝中丹建交65周年,应丹麦驻华大使邀请,他历经半年多时间,经过100多道工序,运用几十种

indulged in lacquer art creation, and formed his own school. It can not only allow people to appreciate the elegant cultural atmosphere and quiet and elegant artistic taste of contemporary artists but also feel the nourishment and infiltration of traditional culture. His representative work *Fishing Songs at Dusk* won the National Art Cup Gold Award at the China Arts and Crafts Boutique Expo. *Spring Snow* was collected by the China National Arts and Crafts Museum. *Prayer of a Young Girl* was selected into the 6th "JC Jacobsen" Portrait Competition and toured in art museums in multiple European countries... Many glories have given him more confidence to move towards the world. Go out, and the world is right in front of you. To celebrate the 65th anniversary of the establishment of diplomatic relations between China and Denmark, at the invitation of the Danish Ambassador to China, he spent more than half a year and went through more than 100 procedures, using dozens of natural materials to carefully create lacquer painting portraits of Queen Margrethe II of Denmark and Prince Henrik. Invite in, and in front of you is the world. Fan Fu'an said with a smile that he has taught many foreign apprentices, and John, an American guy, is one of them. Regarding Huizhou lacquer art, the magical change of colors made John sigh, "Half is from nature, and half is from humans." After more than two years of study, he gave the young man a cultural and creative pen of Huizhou lacquer art to promote exchanges and mutual learning among civilizations.

迎客天下
YING KE TIAN XIA

天然材料，精心创作丹麦女王玛格丽特二世和亨里克亲王的漆画肖像作品。请进来，眼前就是世界。范福安笑言，他教了多名"洋徒弟"，美国小伙约翰即是其一。对徽州漆艺，颜色的魔变让约翰感叹"天一半，人一半"。2 年多学习结束，范福安赠他徽州漆艺文创钢笔，使文化交流互鉴。

国家级非遗"徽州板凳龙"传承人

徽州板凳龙，因龙身为特制的板凳首尾相连而得名。传说龙能行云布雨、消灾降福，故民间多以舞龙祈求平安和丰收。舞板凳龙是流传于徽州的民间舞蹈，是徽州民俗文化中的一朵奇葩。

张光武，徽州板凳龙（右龙板凳龙）省级非遗代表性传承人。2005 年，时年 35 岁的右龙村村主任张光武作为家族的传承人承担起了恢复板凳龙的重任。在族中长辈及父亲的回忆下，张光武根据家中保存的片纸记录恢复了龙首龙尾，组织村民重塑龙身，并借鉴其他龙狮表演的动作和技术，由其本人担任龙首，整合排练右龙板凳龙的表演，一舞成功，使右龙板凳龙文化得到了历史的传承，再创了板凳龙的辉煌。现在，每年元宵节，徽州深山右龙板凳龙的表演深深吸引着民俗爱好者。2008 年张光武带领右龙板凳龙跨出省界赴江西瑶里参加"江西省瑶里茶文化旅游节"表演，震撼全场。

The Inheritor of the National Intangible Cultural Heritage "Huizhou Bench Dragon"

Huizhou Bench Dragon gets its name because the dragon body is formed by connecting the special benches end to end. Legend has it that the dragon can make clouds and rain, eliminate disasters and bring blessings. Therefore, the folk often perform the dragon dance to pray for peace and a good harvest. The Bench Dragon Dance is a folk dance spread in Huizhou and is a wonderful flower in Huizhou folk culture.

Zhang Guangwu is a provincial-level intangible cultural heritage representative inheritor of Huizhou Bench Dragon (Youlong Bench Dragon). In 2005, Zhang Guangwu, the 35-year-old village director of Youlong Village at that time, as the family's inheritor, shouldered the heavy responsibility of restoring the Bench Dragon. With the memories of the elders in the clan and his father, Zhang Guangwu restored the dragon head and tail according to the fragmentary records preserved at home, organized the villagers to reshape the dragon body, and drew on the movements and techniques of other dragon and lion performances. He played the role of the dragon head, integrated and rehearsed the performance of the Youlong Bench Dragon, which was a success at one stroke, enabling the Youlong Bench Dragon culture to be passed down in history and creating new glories for the Bench Dragon. After three years of inheritance and innovation, in 2008, Zhang Guangwu led the Youlong Bench Dragon to cross the provincial border to Yaoli in Jiangxi to participate

迎客天下
YING KE TIAN XIA

王茂荫：《资本论》里提到的唯一的中国人

在人文徽州的历史中，徽州名人及他们对徽州文化的贡献是非常重要的部分。在中国式现代化的黄山故事里，被吴晗誉为"清代货币改革家"的王茂荫无疑是诸多名人中最璀璨者之一。

王茂荫（1798—1865），字椿年，号子怀，清代财政学家。歙县杞梓里人，后移居雄村义成。清道光十二年（1832年）进士，历任户部主事、御史、户部右侍郎、左副都御史、工部侍郎、吏部右侍郎等职务。王茂荫在京历任三朝，居官30年，不携眷属随任，一直独居宣武门外歙县会馆，以两袖清风、直言敢谏闻名。1864年，因为母亲去世离职返乡，1865年在家乡病逝。

清咸丰元年（1851年），54岁的王茂荫进入政坛高光时期，八月，被清廷补授陕西道监察御史，从五品，既是言官，也从事财政工作。当年，太平天国运动爆发，导致"滇铜"运输中断和战争军饷剧增，清财政危机加剧。

为缓解"钱荒"，王茂荫上奏了《条议钞法折》，向咸丰皇帝提出了发行纸币的主张和十条币制改革措施，但未被采纳。然而，咸丰三年（1853年）开始实

in the performance at the Jiangxi Yaoli Tea Culture Tourism Festival and shocked the whole audience.

Wang Maoyin: the Only Chinese Mentioned in *Capital*

In the history of humanistic Huizhou, celebrities and their contributions to Huizhou culture are very important. In the Huangshan stories of Chinese modernization, Wang Maoyin, hailed as the "reformer of the currency system in the Qing Dynasty" by Wu Han, is undoubtedly one of the most brilliant among many celebrities.

Wang Maoyin (1798−1865), with the courtesy name Chunnian and the art name Zihuai, was a financial scientist in the Qing Dynasty. He was from Qizili in Shexian County and later moved to Yicheng in Xiongcun Village. He passed the imperial examination in 1832 during the reign of Daoguang in the Qing Dynasty and successively held positions such as the director of the Ministry of Revenue, censor, right vice minister of the Ministry of Revenue, left deputy censor-in-chief, vice minister of the Ministry of Works, and right vice minister of the Ministry of Personnel. Wang Maoyin served in the capital during three dynasties. He held official positions for 30 years without bringing his family along with him. He always lived alone in the Shexian Guild Hall outside Xuanwu Gate and was famous for his incorruptibility and bold remonstrance. In 1864, he resigned and returned to his

迎客天下
YING KE TIAN XIA

行发钞、铸大钱措施，王茂荫的兑现主张被否定，结果引起纸币严重贬值，民意沸腾。王茂荫坚决反对这一切，一再上书指陈其弊，但始终未被皇帝采纳。咸丰四年（1854年），王茂荫上《再议钞法折》，咸丰帝阅后龙颜大怒，申饬王茂荫专受商人指使，下令撤销了他的户部右侍郎兼管钱法堂事务之职，调补兵部右侍郎。

王茂荫（王茂荫六世孙王铁提供。曹天生 摄）
Wang Maoyin (Photo by Cao Tiansheng, provided by Wang Tie, the sixth-generation descendant of Wang Maoyin)

hometown due to the death of his mother and passed away in his hometown in 1865.

In the first year of Xianfeng (1851), the 54-year-old Wang Maoyin entered the highlight period of his political career. In August, he was appointed as the censor of the Shaanxi Circuit by the Qing court. He held the fifth-rank official position. He was both a remonstrating official and engaged in financial work. In that year, the Taiping Heavenly Kingdom Movement broke out, which led to the interruption of the "Yunnan Copper" transportation and a sharp increase in war military pay, and the financial crisis of the Qing Dynasty intensified.

To alleviate the coin shortage, Wang Maoyin presented the *Memorial on the Discussion of the Paper Currency Law*, proposing to Emperor Xianfeng the idea of issuing paper currency and ten measures for currency system reform, but it was not adopted. However, in the third year of Xianfeng (1853), the measures of issuing paper currency and casting large-denomination coins were implemented. Wang Maoyin's proposal for currency redemption was rejected, resulting in a serious devaluation of paper currency and public outcry. Wang Maoyin firmly opposed all this and repeatedly submitted memorials pointing out the drawbacks, but his views were never adopted by the emperor. In the fourth year of Xianfeng (1854), Wang Maoyin presented the *Memorial on the Re-discussion of the Paper Currency Law*. After reading it, Emperor Xianfeng flew into a rage and reprimanded Wang Maoyin for being under the instigation of merchants. He

迎客天下
YING KE TIAN XIA

王茂荫的"严行申饬"事件,被俄国驻北京布道团第13班的修士大司祭巴拉第得知,他立即从清廷搜集到王茂荫的奏折等有关材料,并让他的下属编译成俄文,然后将之编入《帝俄驻北京布道团人员论著集刊》第三卷,该卷于1857年出版。1858年该书又被德国人卡尔·阿伯尔和弗·阿·梅克伦堡译成德文版发行,马克思在写作《资本论》过程中看到了这本书。马克思对王茂荫的货币观点是赞同的,他在《1857—1858年经济学手稿》中就这样说过:"如果纸币以金银命名,这就说明它应该能换成它所代表的金银的数量,不管它在法律上是否可以兑现。一旦纸币不再是这样,它就会贬值。"于是有了那个标号为83的注释,王茂荫成为马克思在《资本论》中提到的唯一的中国人。

ordered the revocation of Wang Maoyin's position as the right vice minister of the Ministry of Revenue in charge of the affairs of the Money Law Hall and transferred him to be the right vice minister of the Ministry of War.

The incident of Wang Maoyin being severely reprimanded was learned by Father Palladius, the Archimandrite of the 13th Class of the Russian Mission in Beijing. He immediately collected relevant materials such as Wang Maoyin's memorials from the Qing court and asked his subordinate to compile and translate them into Russian. The materials were then included in Volume 3 of *the Collection of Works by the Personnel of the Russian Mission in Beijing*, which was published in 1857. In 1858, this book was translated into German by K. Abel and F. A. Mecklenburg and released in German version. K. Marx read this book during the process of writing *Capital*. K. Marx agreed with Wang Maoyin's monetary views. As he said in the *Economic Manuscripts of 1857–1858*: "If paper money is named after gold and silver, it indicates that it should be able to be exchanged for the amount of gold and silver it represents, regardless of whether it is legally redeemable. Once the paper money is no longer like this, it will depreciate." Thus, in the note numbered 83, Wang Maoyin became the only Chinese mentioned by K. Marx in *Capital*.

一江好水
一城秀美

黄山市山水资源丰富，全市森林覆盖率达82.9%，地表水质较优，是华东地区重要的生态屏障。黄山市始终坚持绿水青山就是金山银山的理念，守护好一片青山，一江清水，在生态文明建设上展示出"生态强市"该有的本色。

Clean River
Beautiful City

Huangshan City has rich natural resources, with a forest coverage rate of 82.9% and relatively clean surface water quality. It is an important ecological barrier in East China. Huangshan City has always adhered to the concept of "Green is gold", guarding its green mountains and clean water, and showcasing the true nature of an "ecological outstanding city" in ecological civilization construction.

迎客天下
YING KE TIAN XIA

在黄山市尊重自然、顺应自然、保护自然的过程中，诞生了许多先进经验和做法：始终坚持良好的生态环境是最普惠的民生福祉，建设秀美之城；皖浙两省"亿元对赌"，共同保护好新安江；"中国好人"日夜守护着迎客松，让中国绿都更加名副其实。

"现代城市"到"秀美之城"

为让居民和游客都能从城市良好生态中获益，黄山市进行了大量探索：建设各具特色的"口袋公园"，走出家门就可休息锻炼；打造全国最干净城市，席地而坐成为日常；保护好城市中的生态湿地，成为最亮眼名片。

高山上看屯溪（凌蔚强 摄）

Viewing Tunxi from Geshan Mountain (Photo by Ling Weiqiang)

In the process of respecting, conforming to, and protecting nature in Huangshan City, many advanced experiences and practices have emerged: We have always insisted that a good ecological environment is the most inclusive public welfare, and we strive to build a beautiful city; Anhui and Zhejiang provinces have "billion-yuan bet" on protecting the Xin'an River together; "the Good People of China" are guarding the Guest-Greeting Pine around the clock, making China's Green City even more deserving of its name.

A Beautiful Modern City

To benefit both residents and tourists from the city's good ecology, Huangshan City has made many explorations: building pocket parks with distinctive features, where residents can rest and exercise just by stepping out of their homes; creating the cleanest city in the country, where sitting on the ground, has become a daily routine; protecting the city's ecological wetlands, which have become the most eye-catching card.

Wasteland Turned into "Pocket Parks"

Under the setting sun, a series of small parks surrounded by green trees are in harmony with tall buildings, residential areas, and bridges, forming a beautiful picture. Why are these parks in the city so small and beautiful? Where do they come from and what role do they play? These parks, also known

迎客天下
YING KE TIAN XIA

荒地变"口袋公园"

夕阳下,绿树环抱的一个个小公园与高楼、小区、大桥等交相辉映,构成一幅美丽的画卷。这些公园为何如此小而美?又从何而来,有何作用?这些公园,又名"口袋公园",是城市微更新的一项重要内容,能够为周围群众提供一个休闲的好去处。黄山市的"口袋公园"大多脱胎于城市里一些难以利用的"边角料"土地,依托"微改造、精提升",把道路拐角,灌木丛等碎片空间改造成一个个特色鲜明的"口袋公园"。不仅绿化城市,提升城市颜值,也为市民提供了出家门就可以游玩的场所,做到了可游、可赏、可玩。

夏季刚到,位于休宁县横江路和新安路交会处的东湖公园就热闹了起来,周边的居民纷纷到公园里散步、带娃。东湖公园原本是居民区附近的一片荒地,杂草丛生。这一片区域原本没有公园,居民渴望能有一个休闲娱乐的场地。于是,在政府的牵头下,把这片荒地改造成了小公园,既美化了环境,也能满足人民群众的现实需要。改造后的东湖公园集休闲、健身、娱乐为一体,不仅有各种运动器材,还建设了重檐六角亭、长廊等。整个公园的内容更加多元化,已然成为附近居民休闲娱乐的首选地点,为喧哗的都市提供了一个安静的城市绿洲。

"口袋公园"除了能够提供健身、休闲的场地之外,

as "pocket parks", are an important part of urban micro-renovation, providing a good place for people to relax around them. Most of the "pocket parks" in Huangshan City are born from the "leftover" land in the city that is difficult to utilize, relying on "micro-renovation and fine enhancement" to transform the road corners, shrubbery, and other fragmented spaces into distinctive "pocket parks" that not only green the city and enhance the city's appearance level, but also provide a place for citizens to play and enjoy within walking distance of their homes.

The summer has just begun, and the East Lake Park located at the intersection of Hongjiang Road and Xin'an Road in Xiuning County is bustling with activity. Residents from the surrounding areas have flocked to the park to take a leisurely stroll and spend time with their children. The East Lake Park used to be a patch of wasteland near a residential area, overgrown with weeds. There was no park in this area, and residents longed for a place to relax and have fun. So, with the government's initiative, the wasteland was transformed into a small park, not only beautifying the environment but also meeting the people's practical needs. The East Lake Park renovated integrates leisure, fitness, and entertainment. In addition to various sports equipment, the park also features a double-eaved hexagonal pavilion and a covered walkway. The park has become more diverse, and it has already become the preferred leisure and entertainment spot for nearby residents, providing a peaceful urban oasis

迎客天下
YING KE TIAN XIA

是否还能满足群众在文化方面的需要？屯溪方言公园给出了答案。此处原本是老旧的市民游园，破损较多，鲜有居民游玩。在政府的主导下，这里被更新打造成"徽州方言"主题公园。公园整体规划设置儿童游乐区和健身活动区，也有景观休闲亭、风雨长廊等休憩场所，同时利用坐凳、挡墙、转角展示方言小品，安装方言墙和触摸显示屏，全面展示徽州方言的相关内容，

屯溪方言公园（凌蔚强　摄）
Tunxi Dialect Park (Photo by Ling Weiqiang)

amidst the hustle and bustle of the city.

In addition to providing fitness and leisure spaces, can "pocket parks" also meet the cultural needs of the public? Tunxi Dialect Park has answered this question. It used to be an old municipal park for residents, with many damages and few visitors. Under the leadership of the government, it was transformed into a "Huizhou Dialect" themed park. The park is planned in a comprehensive manner, with children's play areas and fitness activity zones, as well as scenic pavilions, covered walkways, and other resting places. At the same time, the park uses benches, retaining walls, and corner displays to showcase dialect-themed skits, and installs "dialect walls" and touch screen displays to fully showcase the related content of Huizhou dialect, increasing the fun and interactivity. Children have felt the charm of dialect here, which is also the best introduction to Huizhou culture.

Huangshan City's Xiuning East Lake Park and Tunxi Dialect Park are just a snapshot of the city's efforts to build "pocket parks". In recent years, Huangshan City has implemented urban refinement with a gradual and incremental approach, transforming vacant land, idle land, road nodes, and unused green spaces into beautiful parks. The city is "filling in the gaps" with greenery to meet the growing need of citizens to enjoy beautiful scenery outside their homes.

Sit on the Ground

Walking and stopping in Tunxi, from the ancient

迎客天下
YING KE TIAN XIA

增加趣味性和互动性。小朋友在这里感受方言的魅力,是徽州文化最好的启蒙。

休宁东湖公园和屯溪方言公园只是黄山市建设"口袋公园"的一个缩影。近年来,黄山市以小规模、渐进式的手法实施城市精细化建设,将城市腾退地、闲置土地、道路节点、街角无功能绿地等全面提升,"见缝插绿",不断满足人民群众出门见景的美好生活需要。

席地而坐

在屯溪走走停停,从湖边古村落一路走到黄口桥头。游客刘女士赞叹道:"屯溪确实是一个美好的小城市,我刚下高铁就发现这里的空气非常清新,而且天空也非常蓝!真的是童年记忆里的蓝天。"刘女士在来黄山之前已经做好了旅游攻略,不仅去了黄山、宏村等旅游景点,还特意到市区走走。"我们刚刚从湖边古村落那个方向走过来,一路上看了新安江大好山水,累了就坐在公园的凳子上,甚至是草坪上。"刘女士又感叹道:"黄山这座城市真的是非常干净,可以用一尘不染来形容了!"黄山之所以如此干净,是因为市政府始终坚持干净是看得见、摸得着的,也是和人民群众生活息息相关的,一座现代化的城市一定是一个干干净净的城市。刘女士回到酒店之后,和酒店老板聊起了一天的所见。老板笑着说道:"黄山本来就是一个旅

village by the lake all the way to Huangkou Qiaotou. Ms. Liu, a tourist, exclaimed, "Tunxi is indeed a beautiful small city. I noticed the fresh air and blue sky as soon as I got off the high-speed train. It's the blue sky I remember from my childhood." Ms. Liu had already made a good travel strategy before coming to Huangshan. She not only went to Mount Huangshan, Hongcun and other tourist attractions, but also made a special trip to the city. "We just walked from the lake in that direction of the ancient village, all the way to see the Xin'an River great landscape. When we are tired we just sit on a park bench, or even on the lawn." Ms. Liu exclaimed again "Huangshan City is really very clean and can be described as spotless." The reason why Huangshan City is so clean is that the government has always insisted that cleanliness is visible, tangible, and related to the people's lives, and a modernized city must be a clean city. After Ms. Liu returned to the hotel, she talked to the hotel owner about what she had seen. The owner said with a smile, "Huangshan is originally a tourist city. We want tourists to have fun. 'Clean' is the first impression. Sweeping the road and park clean, picking up the garbage, which has become the norm of our life. Especially since 2022, the cleanliness of the standard is more stringent, and the requirement is to be able to sit on the ground."

"Sitting on the ground", what the hotel owner said, is an important indicator for Huangshan City to create the cleanest city in the country in the action plan. "Sitting on the ground"

迎客天下
YING KE TIAN XIA

一尘不染的呈坎村（凌蔚强 摄）
Clean Chengkan Village (Photo by Ling Weiqiang)

游强市，想要游客们玩得开心，干净是第一印象，把路面和公园扫干净，看到垃圾主动捡起来，已经成为我们生活的常态了，尤其是 2022 年以来，对干净的标准更加严格了，要求能做到席地而坐呢！"

酒店老板所说的"席地而坐"，正是黄山市打造"全国最干净城市"行动计划中的一项重要指标。"席地而坐"就是要求所有可供休息的设施保持随时可坐的卫生状态。这一标准的推进进一步提升了黄山市景区环境卫生治理体系现代化能力和水平，为市民和游客营造了干净、整齐、舒适的生活旅游环境，增加了文旅消费过程中的感受度、体验度和获得感。

is to require all rest facilities to maintain a state of hygiene ready to sit. The promotion of this standard has further enhanced the modernization capabilities and level of the environmental sanitation governance system in Huangshan City's scenic areas, creating a clean, orderly, and comfortable tourism environment for citizens and tourists, and increasing the sense of perception, experience, and fulfilling during the cultural and tourism consumption process.

Mudflats Become "Ecological Wetlands"

Tunxi Sanjiang Provincial Wetland Park consists of rivers, beaches, landscape and greens, including Hengjiang River, Shuaishui River and Xin'an River within the territory of Tunxi District, and is an important permanent river wetland in Tunxi District. The park is distributed along both sides of the river, among which, the westernmost Meilin Wetland Park is often mentioned. Meilin Wetland Park contains a large number of lawns, and after remediation, the environment continues to improve. After a spring rain, Meilin Wetland Park is full of spring, attracting tourists to enjoy spring and trekking. At the turn of spring and summer, a large number of tourists will gather in Meilin Wetland Park to camp, take photos and take a walk. In summer, the park is full of greenery, and lawns, birds, tourists and trees playing a wonderful music of harmony between man and nature. In fall and winter, the redwood forest becomes the brightest spot in the city and the most suitable camping site under the warm winter sun. The increasing improvement of the wetland

迎客天下
YING KE TIAN XIA

滩涂成"生态湿地"

屯溪三江省级湿地公园由河流、滩地、园林、绿地等组成,包含屯溪区境内的横江、率水和新安江,是屯溪区重要的永久性河流湿地。三江省级湿地公园沿着江水两岸分布,其中,大家经常提到的是最西边的梅林湿地公园。梅林湿地公园内有大量的草坪,经过整治之后,环境持续提升。一场春雨过后,梅林湿地公园春意盎然,吸引游人前来赏春踏青。到了春夏之交,梅林湿地公园里便会聚集大量游客露营、拍照、散步。夏天,这里满眼绿意,草坪、小鸟、游客、大树奏响人与自然和谐相处的美妙乐章。秋冬季节,红杉林成为城市中最亮眼的打卡点,成为冬日暖阳下最合适的露营场地。湿地生态环境的日益改善也为黄山市增添了许多生机与活力。

黄山市湿地保护为何如此之好?这是因为黄山市一直高度重视对湿地生态的修复和保护,把湿地公园建设列为林长制目标责任考核的重要内容,注重加强宣传教育,让全社会都参与到湿地保护中来。休宁县农民吴永富家有两株红豆杉,他拒绝了外地客商高价购买的请求,将其无偿捐赠给了休宁横江湿地公园。他说:"在这里,红豆杉的生长环境、受到的保护都比在我家好。能为休宁的城市生态发展作一点贡献,我感到很开心。"2023年5月,以"保护全球候鸟迁徙通

ecological environment has also added a lot of vitality and vigor to Huangshan City.

Why is the wetland protection so good? Because Huangshan City has always attached great importance to the restoration and protection of wetland ecology, and has listed the construction of wetland parks as an important content of the target responsibility assessment for the forestry chief system. It pays attention to strengthening publicity and education, so that the whole society can participate in wetland protection. In Xiuning County, farmer Wu Yongfu's family has two yew trees. He refused the request of merchants to buy them at a high price, and donated them to Xiuning Hengjiang Wetland Park. He said: "Here, the growing environment and protection received by the yew trees are better than my home. I feel happy to make a little contribution to the urban ecological development of Xiuning." In May 2023, the "Bird Preservation Week" nature notes activity with the theme of "Protecting Global Migratory Birds' Migratory Corridors" was officially launched in Xiuning Hengjiang Wetland Park, where young people were led by wetland staff to learn about wetland and bird protection. Nowadays, Hiuning Hengjiang Wetland Park has become a "nature textbook", attracting residents and young people to pay attention to the wetland and protect the wetland. The protection of Huangshan wetland parks is becoming more and more efficient under the joint efforts of government-led and public participation.

迎客天下
YING KE TIAN XIA

道"为主题的"爱鸟周"自然笔记活动在休宁横江湿地公园正式启动，青少年们在湿地工作人员的带领下学习湿地和鸟类保护相关知识。如今的休宁横江湿地公园已经成为"自然教科书"，吸引着居民朋友和青少年们投入到关注湿地、保护湿地的工作中来。在政府主导和公众参与的共同努力下，黄山湿地公园的保护也越来越高效。

"新安江水"到"一江好水"

皖浙两省"亿元对赌"，只为保护好新安江水，开创用垃圾兑换生活用品先河的生态美超市，新安江渔民上岸后在政府帮助下适应"岸上生活"。黄山市正让更多居民切身体会到良好生态带来的美好。

"亿元对赌"赌出优质江水

一江碧水出新安，百转千回下钱塘。发源于休宁县境内六股尖的新安江，是徽州人民的母亲河，哺育了一代又一代徽州人民，也是长三角重要战略水源地之一。新安江干流总长359公里，近2/3在安徽境内，经黄山市歙县街口镇进入浙江境内，流入下游千岛湖、富春江，汇入钱塘江。千岛湖超过68%的水源来自新安江，新安江水质优劣很大程度决定了千岛湖的水质好坏。因此，对于浙江杭州而言，希望江水不受污染，

The Clean Water of Xin'an River

To protect the Xin'an River, Anhui and Zhejiang provinces have "billion-yuan bet" on it, aiming to protect the river water and pioneer the use of trash for exchange of daily necessities at an eco-beauty supermarket. After leaving the river, fishermen from Xin'an River are adapting to "land life" with the help of the government, and Huangshan City is letting more residents experience the beauty brought by good ecology.

"Billion-Yuan Bet" Secures High-Quality River Water

A crystal-clear river flows out of Xin'an, winding its way through countless bends and turns before reaching Qiantang River. Xin'an River, originating from Liugujian in Xiuning County, is the mother river of the Huizhou people and has nourished generations. It is also one of the important strategic water sources in the Yangtze River Delta region. The total length of Xin'an River main stream is 359 kilometers, nearly 2/3 in the territory of Anhui, through the Jiekou Town, Shexian County, into the territory of Zhejiang, into the downstream of the Qiandao Lake, the Fuchun River, into the Qiantang River. Qiandao Lake has more than 68% of the water from the Xin'an River. The water quality of Xin'an River largely determines the water quality of Qiandao Lake. Therefore, Hangzhou City, Zhejiang Province hopes that

迎客天下
YING KE TIAN XIA

以持续性地获得优质的水源供给。但对于经济后进的黄山而言，更加迫切的愿望是经济发展提速。开展新安江大保护就意味着需要放弃很多发展的机会，群众经济收入也会受到相应影响。如何统筹好上下游之间的利益？2011年，习近平同志作出重要批示，"千岛湖是我国极为难得的优质水资源，加强千岛湖水资源保护意义重大，在这个问题上要避免重蹈先污染后治理的覆辙"，希望"浙江、安徽两省要着眼大局，从源头控制污染，走互利共赢之路"。

在财政部、原环境保护部的推动和皖浙两省的共

新安江（樊成柱 摄）
Xin'an River (Photo by Fan Chengzhu)

the river water can be free from pollution to continuously access to high-quality water supply. But for Huangshan with backward economic, the more urgent desire is to speed up economic development. To carry out the Xin'an River protection means that it needs to give up a lot of development opportunities, and the masses' economic income will also be affected accordingly. How to integrate the interests of upstream and downstream? In 2011, Xi Jinping made an important instruction, "Qiandao Lake is China's extremely rare high-quality water resources. To strengthen the protection of water resources in Qiandao Lake is of great significance. In this issue, it is a need to avoid repeating the mistake of first pollution and then governance. Zhejiang and Anhui should focus on the overall situation, control pollution from the source, and take the road of mutual benefit under win-win situation."

Under the push of the Ministry of Finance and the former Ministry of Environmental Protection, as well as the joint efforts of Anhui and Zhejiang provinces, Xin'an River Basin Ecological Compensation Mechanism Pilot was officially launched to start the "billion-yuan bet". 2012−2014 is the first round of the pilot: for compensation funds, there were cumulative total of 1.5 billion yuan in three years, of which the central government contributed 300 million yuan per year, Anhui and Zhejiang contributed respectively 100 million yuan per year. For assessment method, if the water quality of cross-border's cross section in Anhui and Zhejiang

迎客天下
YING KE TIAN XIA

同努力下,新安江流域生态补偿机制试点正式启动,开启"亿元对赌"。2012—2014年是首轮试点:补偿资金上,三年累计15亿元,其中中央财政每年出资3亿元,安徽、浙江两省每年分别出资1亿元;考核方式上,如果皖浙两省跨界断面水质达到考核标准,浙江省给安徽省1亿元,反之,安徽省给浙江省1亿元。2016年12月签订第二轮生态保护补偿协议。2012—2018年先后两期共6年试点工作,建立起跨省流域横向生态保护补偿机制。2018年皖浙两省第三次签订补偿协议,逐步建立常态化补偿机制。三轮对赌金额总计56亿元,只为一江清水。2023年两省又签订了第四轮协议。"亿元对赌"成效十分显著,新安江水质持续好转,新安江上游流域水质总体为优并稳定向好,已经成为全国水质排名前列的河流,每年向千岛湖输送近70亿立方米干净水,皖浙两省实现双赢。

人不负青山,青山定不负人。从"试点"到"样板",从资金补偿到产业协作。从协同治理到共同发展。浙皖两省不断创新跨省流域生态补偿机制,努力实现从"一水共护"迈向"一域共富"。

"小小积分"兑出美好环境

守护好新安江水,不仅需要依靠皖浙两省政府的共同努力,还需要吸引广大人民群众参与到日常生态环境的保护工作当中。

meets the assessment standard, Zhejiang Province should give 100 million yuan to Anhui Province, otherwise, Anhui Province should give 100 million yuan to Zhejiang Province. The second round of the eco-protection compensation agreement was signed in December 2016. The pilot work of the two successive phases of six years from 2012 to 2018, established the cross-provincial basin horizontal ecological protection compensation mechanism. In 2018, Anhui and Zhejiang signed the compensation agreement for the third time, and gradually established a regularized compensation mechanism. Three rounds of betting amounted to 5.6 billion yuan, just for a river of clear water. In 2023, the two provinces signed the fourth round of agreements. The effect of the "billion-yuan bet" is very significant. The water quality of Xin'an River continues to improve, and the water quality of the upper basin is generally excellent and stable, and has ranked the top in the country, every year to deliver nearly 7 billion cubic meters of clean water to Qiandao Lake. The two provinces have achieved a win-win situation.

If we do not fail Nature, Nature shall never fail us. From "pilot" to "model", from financial compensation to industrial collaboration, from collaborative governance to common development, Zhejiang and Anhui continue to innovate cross-provincial watershed ecological compensation mechanism, and strive to realize from "a water common protection" towards "a common wealth".

迎客天下
YING KE TIAN XIA

新安江的一江碧水(樊成柱 摄)

The clean water of Xin'an River (Photo by Fan Chengzhu)

随着新安江生态补偿协议的签订，作为上游的流口镇，如何更加有效地保护好新安江，成为亟待解决的一个难题。流口镇积极探索，勇于创新，2016年7月，黄山市第一家"垃圾兑换超市"正式营业，后更名为"生态美超市"。生态美超市很特殊，里面的东西不能直接购买，而是需要用积分兑换。村民把日常生活中产生的不易降解和处理、容易造成环境污染的垃圾集中处理，根据兑换标准即可获得相应的积分。在这个过程中，村民获得了实实在在的物品，也吸引更

"Small Points" for a Better Environment

To guard the water of Xin'an River, we not only need to rely on the joint efforts of the governments of Anhui and Zhejiang provinces, but also need to attract the participation of the people in the daily protection of the ecological environment.

With the signing of the Xin'an River ecological compensation agreement, as the upper reaches of the Liukou Town, how to protect the Xin'an River more effectively, has become a difficult problem to solve. Liukou Town actively explored and innovated. In July 2016, the city's first "garbage exchange supermarket" officially opened, and was later renamed "eco-beauty supermarket". Eco-beauty supermarket is very special, and the things inside cannot be directly purchased, but need points to exchange. Villagers can centrally treat the garbage generated in their daily life, which is not easy to degrade and can easily result in environmental pollution, and they can get corresponding points according to the exchange standard. In this process, the villagers gained tangible items and attracted more villagers to join in the garbage exchange, leaving the garbage in the bag in the eco-beauty supermarket and bringing edible oil, plastic buckets and other household items. Under the leading role of the eco-beauty supermarket, protecting the environment, not littering and protecting the river has become the habit and consensus of the villagers.

After the establishment of eco-beauty supermarket,

迎客天下
YING KE TIAN XIA

多村民加入垃圾兑换的行列中,把袋子中的垃圾留在生态美超市,把食用油、塑料桶等生活物品带回家。在生态美超市的引领作用下,保护环境,不乱扔垃圾,保护好江水已经成为村民生活的习惯和共识。

生态美超市建立之后,村民们最直接的感受就是村里以前随处可见的垃圾已基本消失,河水里经常漂浮的塑料袋也不见踪影。取而代之的是一个干干净净的村子和一条干干净净的河。生态环境好了,村民们也有了更多去处,村子也更加宜居。在生态美超市的运行过程中,已经不仅仅局限于垃圾兑换积分,生态美超市的内涵也在不断发展,便民服务、环境整治、护河禁渔、志愿服务等不断融入其中,村民参与乡村治理的热情随着"小积分"而不断高涨,越来越多的村民从旁观者成为切实的参与者。

生态美超市也在黄山从试点走向了全面推广,农村生态环境也随着生态美超市的不断扩大越来越好,黄山市正以实际行动守护好新安江。

"渔民上岸"守住新安江水

为保护好这一江清水,保证新安江的水质,2019年11月,《歙县新安江渔民退捕工作实施方案》出台,新安江渔民"退捕上岸"也最终落槌,这也意味着许多世代以捕鱼为生的渔民需要离开他们赖以生存的渔船。

这一年的12月,小凌下完最后一网之后,决定退

the villagers directly feel that the garbage has basically disappeared, which used to be everywhere, and the plastic bags that often floated in the river have disappeared, replaced by a clean village and a clean river. The ecological environment is better, the villagers also have more places to go, and the village has become more livable. The eco-beauty supermarket has not only been limited to garbage exchange points, the connotation of the eco-beauty supermarket is also constantly developing. Convenient services, environmental improvement, river protection and fishing ban, voluntary service and so on are also constantly integrated into it. The enthusiasm of the villagers to participate in the rural governance also continue to rise with the "small points". More and more villagers have become actual participants from bystanders.

The eco-beauty supermarket has been expanded from a pilot project to full-scale promotion in Huangshan City, and the rural ecological environment has become better and better as the eco-beauty supermarket has expanded. Huangshan City is taking concrete actions to protect Xin'an River.

"Fishermen Ashore" Preserving the Water of Xin'an River

In order to protect the river and ensure the water quality of the Xin'an River, in November 2019, "Shexian Xin'an River Fishermen Retirement Implementation Program" was introduced. The retirement of fishermen from Xin'an River had finally been decided, which meant that many fishermen

迎客天下
YING KE TIAN XIA

捕上岸，不再当一个渔民。退捕上岸之后怎么办？这是小凌最为担心的问题，但他也理解，退捕上岸从眼前来看，是有些损失，但是从长远发展的角度来看，受益的是子孙后代。政府也知道像小凌这样的渔民上岸之后，最为担心的就是生活问题，因此在方案实施之前，就深入渔民一线，进行过广泛调研，不断征求意见。最终实施时，不仅给予渔民补偿，而且通过开展各类技能培训，帮助渔民适应岸上生活。小凌在获知有培训之后，第一时间报了名，他选择的是种植类的课程。"以前当渔民，现在当农民，其实也挺好，靠水吃水，靠山吃山嘛。"培训结束后，小凌投入到种植三潭枇杷的工作中。枇杷丰收的时候，小凌非常开心，因为他算了一下，枇杷种植的收入不比当渔民的时候低。

像小凌这样，从渔民转变为农民的不在少数，歙县新安江流域有 1564 名渔民选择退捕转产。自退捕工作开展以来，歙县政府第一时间便开展技能培训，引导大家发展生态农业、生态旅游，保障渔民上岸有出路、就业有门路、生活有保障。

"环境良好"到中国"绿都"

由北京林业大学发起的中国绿都建设评价研究旨在对全国近 300 个地级城市绿色发展情况进行全面分

who had lived by fishing for generations would have to leave their livelihood, the fishing boat.

In December of that year, Xiao Ling decided to retire from fishing and stop being a fisherman after he finished his last net. What would he do after he retired from fishing? This was Xiao Ling's biggest worry, but he also understood that returning to shore would result in some losses in the short term, but in the long term, it would benefit future generations. The government also knew that fishermen like Xiao Ling were most worried about their livelihood after landing, so before the program was implemented, they went into the fishermen, conducted extensive research and continuously consulted. When the program was finally implemented, not only was compensation given to the fishermen, but also they helped the fishermen adapt to onshore life through various types of skills training. Xiao Ling enrolled in the training program as soon as he learned of its availability, and he chose a course in planting. "I used to be a fisherman, but now I'm a farmer, and it's actually quite a good thing. After the training, Xiao Ling put into the work of planting loquats in Santan. When the loquat harvested, Xiao Ling was very happy because he calculated that the income from loquat planting was not lower than that when he was a fisherman.

Like Xiao Ling, many fishermen have transformed into farmers, with 1,564 fishermen in Xin'an River basin, choosing to retire from fishing and switch to other occupations. Since the cage-free fishing project was

迎客天下
YING KE TIAN XIA

析。2023年度绿都建设评价研究报告发布，黄山市位列第七，已连续4年入选中国绿都综合评价前十，成为生态文明建设、人与自然和谐共生的绿色时代榜样，引领全国各地的绿都建设。

绿色的童话世界

黄山市，宛如一颗镶嵌在中国东部的翡翠宝石，森林覆盖率达82.9%、林地面积1111万亩、活立木蓄积量4490万立方米，三项指标均居安徽省前列，地表水环境质量和环境空气质量长年保持在全国前列。2023年黄山市获评中国十大秀美之城、国家低碳城市试点优良城市、国家生态文明建设示范区，是货真价实的天然氧吧。

踏入这片神奇的土地，仿佛进入了一个绿色的童话世界，山脉绵延起伏，森林郁郁葱葱，像一汪绿色海洋。每一片树叶就是一个小型氧气工厂，在阳光的照耀下，通过光合作用，源源不断地为大自然输送着清新的氧气。无论是漫步在古老的村落，还是攀登险峻的山峰，都能让您深深地感受到大自然的魅力。呼吸着那饱含负氧离子的空气，仿佛每一口都能洗净心灵的疲惫，让身心得到彻底的放松和滋养。黄山市，这个天然氧吧，不仅是大自然的恩赐，更是人们心灵的避风港，吸引着无数向往纯净与美好的人。

值得一提的是，黄山风景区空气负氧离子均值每

launched, the government of Shexian County has launched skill training programs to guide people to develop eco-agriculture and eco-tourism, ensuring that fishermen have ways to make living after they leave the water.

The Green City with Favourable Environment

The evaluation research on China's green city construction initiated by Beijing Forestry University aims to provide a comprehensive analysis of the green development of nearly 300 prefecture-level cities across the country. The report on green city construction evaluation in 2023 has been released, and Huangshan City ranks the seventh. It has been included in the top 10 of China's green city comprehensive evaluation for four consecutive years, becoming a model for ecological civilization construction and harmonious coexistence between man and nature in the green era, leading the construction of green cities across the country.

The Green Fairy-Tale World

Huangshan City, like an emerald inlaid in eastern China, has 82.9% of forest coverage, 11.11 million mu of forest land, and 44.9 million cubic meters of standing trees. All three indicators rank in the forefront of Anhui Province, and the surface water and air quality remain in the forefront of the country for years. In 2023, Huangshan City was rated as one of the top ten beautiful cities of China, a national low-carbon city pilot excellent city, and a national ecological

迎客天下
YING KE TIAN XIA

立方厘米常年维持在 2 万个左右，瞬间峰值达到每立方厘米 26.7 万个，高出世界卫生组织规定的空气清新标准 267 倍。近年来，黄山风景区空气质量优良率达到 100%，森林覆盖率高达 98.3%，有高等植物 2385 种，其中国家重点保护植物 37 种。广东深圳游客小王说："黄山的美景四个季节各不一样，一生至少要来四次，这里就像一幅水墨画，随时随地可以呼吸新鲜空气，简直是人间仙境。"

国宝迎客松

黄山市现有古树名木 10458 株，树龄在 500 年以上实施一级保护的古树 267 株，其中最著名的树木非千

迎客松（窦剑　摄）
The Guest-Greeting Pine (Photo by Dou Jian)

civilization construction demonstration area. It is a genuine natural oxygen bar.

Stepping on this magical land, it feels like entering into a green fairy tale world. The mountains rise and fall, and the forests are lush and green, like a vast ocean of greenery. Each leaf is a small oxygen factory, bathed in sunlight, producing fresh oxygen through photosynthesis and continuously supplying it to nature. Whether taking a leisurely stroll through an ancient village or climbing a rugged mountain, you can deeply feel the charm of nature. Breathing the air rich in negative ions, it feels like every breath cleanses the weariness of the soul, allowing the body and mind to fully relax and nourish. Huangshan City, this natural oxygen bar, is not only a gift from nature, but also a haven for people's souls, attracting countless people who yearn for purity and beauty.

It is worth mentioning that the average concentration of negative oxygen ions in the Mount Huangshan Scenic Area is maintained around 20,000 per cubic centimeter all year round, with a peak value of 267,000 per cubic centimeter, which is 267 times higher than the fresh air standard set by the World Health Organization. In recent years, the air quality in Mount Huangshan Scenic Area has reached 100%, and the forest coverage rate is as high as 98.3%. There are 2,385 species of higher plants, including 37 species of nationally protected plants. Tourist Xiao Wang from Shenzhen City, Guangdong Province said, "The scenery of Huangshan is

迎客天下
YING KE TIAN XIA

年迎客松莫属。提到迎客松，无人不知无人不晓，是名副其实的国宝。它生长在黄山玉屏楼左侧、文殊洞之上的青狮石旁，树高约10米，胸围2.05米，枝下高2.54米，树干中部伸出长达7.6米的两大侧枝，恰似一位好客的主人，张开双臂，热情地欢迎五湖四海的宾客来黄山游览。

迎客松作为中华民族热情好客和包容开放的象征，早已扬名中外，成为中国走向世界的一张亮丽名片。1959年，巨幅铁画《迎客松》被放置在北京人民大会堂会见大厅。1994年，国画《迎客松》被悬挂在北京人民大会堂东大厅。2018年，中国山水画《黄山迎客松》作为国礼赠送给东盟秘书处，象征着中国人民开放包容、海纳百川的宽广胸怀。

"中国好人"李培生、胡晓春

2022年8月13日，习近平总书记给"中国好人"李培生、胡晓春回信，对他们"长年在山崖间清洁环境，日复一日呵护着千年迎客松，用心用情守护美丽的黄山"的敬业奉献精神给予充分肯定，对他们继续发挥好"中国好人"榜样作用提出殷切期望。

李培生是黄山风景区的一名放绳工。他和搭档在负责的片区巡查，平均每人每天放绳作业4到5次，且作业的环境很特殊，不是悬崖峭壁，就是荆棘丛林，十分具有挑战性。在黄山风景区所有放绳工中，李培

different in each season, and I should come here at least four times in my lifetime. It's like a watercolor painting, where I can breathe fresh air anytime and anywhere. It's truly a paradise on earth."

National Treasure, the Guest-Greeting Pine

There are 10,458 ancient and famous trees in Huangshan City, and 267 ancient trees with the age of more than 500 years are under primary protection, of which the most famous tree is the millennium Guest-Greeting Pine. When it comes to Guest-Greeting Pine, no one can remain unaware or uninformed. It is indeed a national treasure. It grows on the left side of Mount Huangshan's Yuping Building, above the Wenshu Cave, beside the Qingshi Stone. It is about 10 meters tall, with a trunk circumference of 2.05 meters, a branch clearance of 2.54 meters, and a 7.6-meter-long lateral branch extending from the trunk midsection, like a hospitable host opening the arms to warmly welcome guests from all over the world.

The Guest-Greeting Pine, which serves as a symbol of the Chinese people's warm hospitality and open-mindedness, has long been renowned both at home and abroad, and has become a beautiful calling card. In 1959, the giant iron painting *Guests-Greeting Pine* was placed in the meeting hall of the Great Hall of the People in Beijing. In 1994, the traditional Chinese painting *Guests-Greeting Pine* was hung in the East Hall of the Great Hall of the People in Beijing. In 2018, the Chinese landscape painting *Mount Huangshan Guests-Greeting Pine* was presented to

迎客天下
YING KE TIAN XIA

李培生（樊成柱　摄）

Li Peisheng (Photo by Fan Chengzhu)

生是公认功夫最好的一位。他坚信不能让垃圾破坏了美丽的风景，宁脏一人，不污一处，要以山为家。自1999年以来的25年间，李培生总计放绳长度约等于攀爬了200多次珠穆朗玛峰，其间无责任事故发生。他除了清捡悬崖上的垃圾，还经常帮游客捡拾跌落山间的物品，这让他收获了成就感和幸福感。

胡晓春是黄山迎客松的第19任守松人。2010年，他通过考核选拔，担任第18任守松人的B岗，一年之后，正式成为第19任守松人。每年，他都有300多天吃住在山上，与迎客松朝夕相伴。因为迎客松的重要地位和特殊意义，守护工作需要细致入微。树干、枝

the ASEAN Secretariat as a national gift, symbolizing the broad mind of the Chinese people to be open, inclusive and open to all.

"Good People of China" Li Peisheng and Hu Xiaochun

On August 13, 2022, President Xi Jinping wrote a letter in reply to "Good People of China" Li Peisheng and Hu Xiaochun, fully acknowledging their dedication and professionalism in "cleaning the environment among cliffs for years, caring for the millennium Guests-Greeting Pine day after day, and guarding the beautiful Huangshan with heart and soul", and expressing earnest expectations for them to continue to play an exemplary role as "Good People of China".

Li Peisheng is a rope operator in the Mount Huangshan Scenic Area. He and his partner patrol their designated area, performing rope operations an average of four to five times per person per day. The working environment is particularly challenging, as it often involves treacherous cliffs or dense thorn bushes. Among all the rope operators in the Mount Huangshan Scenic Area, Li Peisheng is widely acknowledged as the most skilled. He firmly believes that garbage should not spoil the beauty of the scenery, and he is willing to get dirty himself to keep the environment clean, treating the mountain as his home. Since 1999, Li Peisheng has accumulated a total rope length equivalent to climbing Mount Qomolangma more than 200 times over the past 25 years, without any accidents occurring during this period. In addition to collecting garbage

迎客天下
YING KE TIAN XIA

胡晓春（樊成柱　摄）

Hu Xiaochun (Photo by Fan Chengzhu)

条和松针上的每个部位都要仔细查看，尤其是要防止病虫害，有异常情况要及时上报。光靠肉眼还不行，必须使用望远镜才能把每一个细节看得很清楚，这是一个考验耐心和细心的工作。每天早上六点半，胡晓春便开始第一次对迎客松的巡查，之后每隔两小时进行一次巡查，并将巡查情况写进《迎客松日记》，把巡护的情况及时详细地填写在上面。13 年内，胡晓春撰写的《迎客松日记》达 70 多本，约 140 万字。

from cliffs, he also frequently helps tourists retrieve items that have fallen into the mountains, which brings him a sense of achievement and happiness.

Hu Xiaochun is the 19th guardian of the Guest-Greeting Pine in Mount Huangshan. In 2010, he passed the assessment and selection to serve as the B-position for the 18th guardian, and a year later, he officially became the 19th guardian. Every year, he spends over 300 days living and working in the mountain, accompanying the pine day and night. Due to the significant status and special meaning of the Guest-Greeting Pine, the guardian's work requires meticulous attention to detail. Every part of the trunk, branches, and pine needles must be carefully inspected, especially to prevent pests and diseases, and any abnormalities must be reported promptly. The naked eye is not enough, and a telescope must be used to see every detail clearly. This is a job that tests patience and carefulness. Every morning at 6:30, Hu Xiaochun begins his first inspection of the pine, followed by inspections every two hours thereafter. He records the inspection details in the *Guest-Greeting Pine Diary*, filling it out promptly and thoroughly with the status of the patrols. During 13 years, Hu Xiaochun has written over 70 volumes of the diary, totaling approximately 1.4 million words.

茶乡山居
香飘万里

在中国式现代化的进程中，我们坚持把实现人民对美好生活的向往作为出发点和落脚点，促进城乡融合发展，刷新黄山形象。这里有黄山毛峰、祁门红茶、太平猴魁等世界名茶，这里有徽菜臭鳜鱼、徽州毛豆腐、黄山烧饼等中国美食，这里有以烟雨朦胧、小桥流水、田园如画等为特色的徽州民宿，这里还有"醉美"公路、高铁枢纽、"空中走廊"等便利交通……让国际友人品黄山名茶，尝徽州美食，住徽州民宿。

Dwelling in Tea Producing Villages

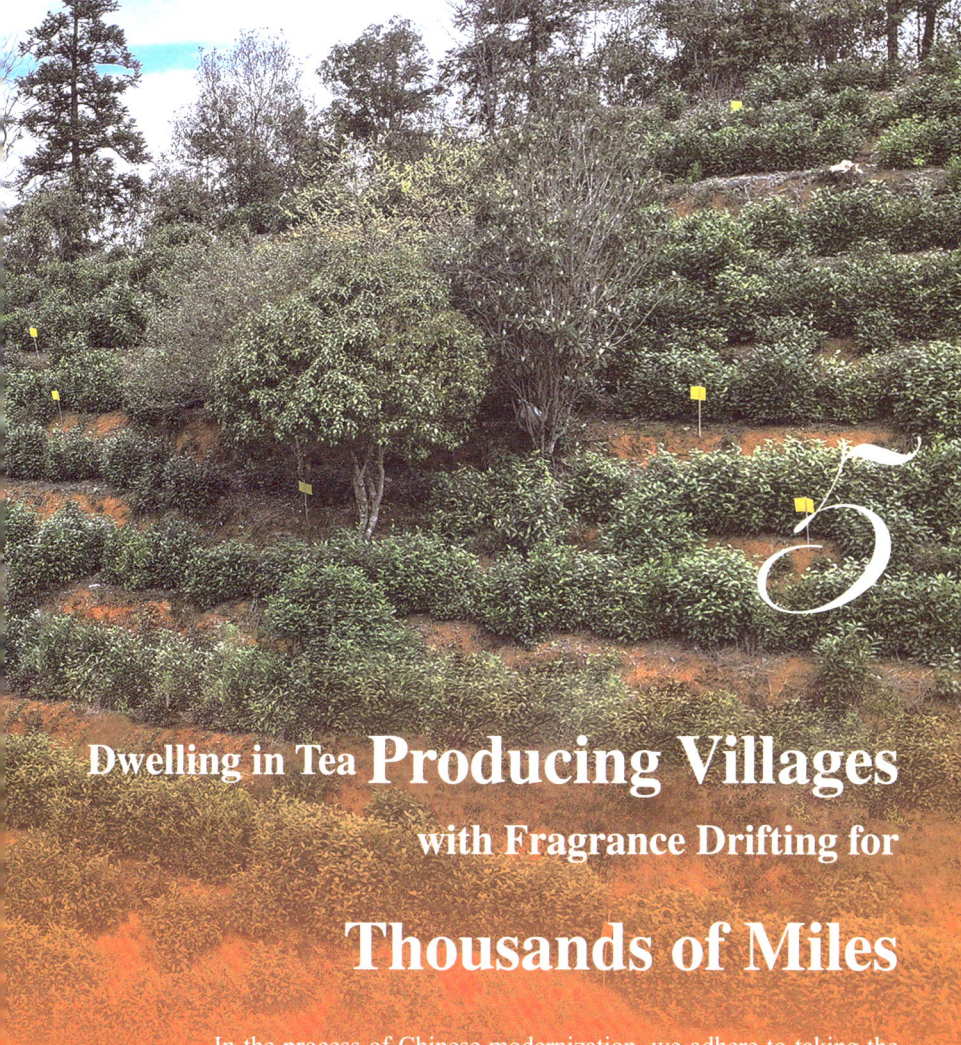

with Fragrance Drifting for

Thousands of Miles

In the process of Chinese modernization, we adhere to taking the realization of people's aspirations for a better life as our starting point and goal, promoting the integration of urban and rural development, and refreshing the image of Huangshan. There are world famous teas such as Mount Huangshan Maofeng, Qimen Black Tea, Taiping Houkui, etc.; there are Chinese delicacies such as Anhui Cuisine stinky mandarin fish, Huizhou Maotofu, Huangshan Shaobing (Baked cake in griddle), etc.; there are Huizhou homestays featuring misty rain, small bridges and flowing water, picturesque countryside, etc., and convenient transportation such as roads, high-speed rail hubs, "air corridors", etc… so that international friends can taste Mount Huangshan famous tea, taste Huizhou cuisine, and live in Huizhou homestays.

迎客天下
YING KE TIAN XIA

茶香四溢

　　黄山地区自然条件独特，它处于北纬 30°的神秘地带，经历了无数的地壳活动和造山运动。长期受雨浸风化作用，山脉地表层以黄棕砂石土壤为主，土层深厚。再加上此地气候温润，雨量充沛，山高林密，云雾缭绕，特别适合茶树的生长。根据唐朝茶圣陆羽的

黄山市茶叶产地（樊成柱　摄）
The producing area of tea in Huangshan City (Photo by Fan Chengzhu)

The Fragrance of Tea Fills the Air

The natural conditions of Mount Huangshan is unique. It is located in the mysterious zone of 30° north latitude, and has experienced numerous crustal activities and orogeny. The mountains are continuously weathered by rain for a long time, making the mountain surface layer mainly yellowish-brown sandstone soil, and the soil layer is deep. In addition, the climate here is warm, with abundant rainfall, high mountains and dense forests, shrouded in clouds and mist, making it particularly suitable for the growth of tea trees. According to the theory of tea sage Lu Yu of the Tang Dynasty, the tea grown on the sand and gravel hills is of the highest quality. Mount Huangshan is in line with such soil conditions. As a national key famous tea producing area, Mount Huangshan has a rich variety of tea, a long history of planting, and mature and developed traditional tea making techniques. It has three top famous teas: Mount Huangshan Maofeng, Qimen Black Tea, and Taiping Houkui.

Make a Cup of Reassuring Tea

Fuxi Township, Huizhou District, is the advantageous production area and the hometown of Mount Huangshan Maofeng. The township's tea garden covers an area of 19,800 mu, with 1,615 tea farmers, 53 tea enterprises and tea industry operators, and 39 enterprises authorized to use the group logo of "Mount Huangshan Maofeng of Fuxi Tea

理论,砂石乱岗上所种的茶是上品。黄山地区正符合这样的土壤条件。作为全国重点名茶产区,黄山茶叶种类丰富,种植历史悠久,传统制茶技艺成熟发达,拥有黄山毛峰、祁门红茶、太平猴魁三大顶流名茶。

做一杯放心茶

徽州区富溪乡是黄山毛峰优势产区、中国黄山毛峰之乡。全乡茶园面积1.98万亩,茶农1615户,茶企、茶业经营主体53家,被授权使用"黄山毛峰富溪产区茶"团体标识的有39家,同时开展溯源秤安装,茶农卡、茶企卡的发放。

位于大山中的富溪村双坑口村村民汪婆婆领到了一张带有二维码的茶农卡,汪婆婆兴奋地说:"我家的粘虫黄板插放到位,茶园不打农药和除草剂,验收合格才会给我发放茶农卡。"在富溪乡,每个茶农师傅脖子上都挂有一张茶农卡。这相当于当地茶农的卖茶"身份证",茶企通过扫描茶农卡二维码,可以清晰掌握茶农所采茶叶的相关信息,以此溯源所收茶叶是否为正宗富溪毛峰小产区茶,从前端确保茶叶质量。

"一张茶农卡,带来的是富溪茶农对黄山毛峰核心产区地位的珍惜与自信。'茶产业大脑'工作开展以来,茶农和茶企对此的接受度越来越高,维护富溪小产区茶品牌和质量的意识进一步增强。"黄山市茶产业发展中心负责人介绍,他们构建茶产业的数字化应用场景,

Production Area". The township carries out the installation of traceability scales and the issuance of tea farmer cards and tea enterprise cards.

Mrs. Wang, a villager from Shuangkengkou Village in Fuxi Village, located in the mountains, received a tea farmer card with a QR code. She said excitedly, "My sticky insect yellow board is inserted in place, and the tea garden does not use pesticides or herbicides. Only after passing the inspection will I be issued a tea farmer card." In Fuxi Township, every tea farmer wears a tea farmer card around their neck. This is equivalent to the "ID card" of local tea farmers to sell tea. Tea companies can scan the QR code of the tea farmer's card to clearly grasp the relevant information of the tea collected by the tea farmers, thereby tracing whether the collected tea is authentic tea from the Fuxi Maofeng small production area, and ensuring the quality of tea from the status.

"A tea farmer's card brings about the cherishing and confidence of Mount Huangshan Maofeng core production status among the tea farmers in Fuxi. Since the work of the 'Tea Industry Brain', has been launched, the acceptance rate among tea farmers and tea enterprises has been increasing, and the awareness of maintaining the brand and quality of the small production area has been further enhanced," the person in charge of Mount Huangshan Tea Industry Development Center introduced. The digital application scenario of the tea industry has been built, and the traceability management platform for Mount Huangshan Maofeng and other famous

迎客天下
YING KE TIAN XIA

并完善黄山毛峰等名茶品牌溯源管理平台，进一步强化茶叶质量安全监管，禁止外来茶叶以次充好，避免"劣币驱逐良币"，稳步提升黄山茶产品溢价能力，持续提高黄山茶品牌价值。

"你们祁红，世界有名"

"你们祁红，世界有名"，邓小平同志1979年登黄山时说。中国祁门红茶与印度大吉岭红茶和斯里兰卡乌伐的季节茶并称为世界三大高香茶。

1915年，祁门红茶在巴拿马太平洋国际博览会上获得金奖，之后多次在国际上获得金奖，特别是在2020年获第105届巴拿马万国博览会"特等金奖"。

2022年中国传统制茶技艺及其相关习俗成功列入《人类非物质文化遗产代表作名录》，其中祁门红茶制作技艺成功入选。传统的祁门红茶依靠手工制作，质量好坏取决于手上功夫，因此祁门红茶又叫"祁门工夫"。祁门红茶制作技艺分为初制和精制两大部分。初制是将鲜叶制成毛茶，包括萎凋、揉捻、发酵、干燥等工序。鲜叶在初制加工前，要进行分级，使原料均匀一致，防止老嫩、劣杂混在一起，初制成的茶叶叫毛茶，必须经过精制，才能成为商品茶。精制的目的是整饬形状，分类等级，剔除夹杂物，减除水分，缩小体积，便于包装贮运，以符合各级标准样茶的规格要求。精制包括筛分、切断、风选、拣剔、拼配、复

tea brands has been built to further strengthen the supervision of tea quality and safety, prohibit other tea from shoddy, avoid "bad money expelling good money", steadily improve the premium ability of Mount Huangshan tea products, and continue to improve Mount Huangshan tea brand value.

Qimen Black Tea Is World-Renowned

"The Qihong (Qimen Black Tea) is world famous," said Deng Xiaoping when he climbed Mount Huangshan in 1979. Qimen Black Tea of China, along with Darjeeling Black Tea of India and Uva Seasonal Tea of Sri Lanka, is known as the three major high aroma teas in the world.

In 1915, Qimen Black Tea won a gold medal at the Panama International Exposition, and won multiple gold medals internationally later, especially the Special Gold Award at the 105th Panama International Exposition in 2020.

In 2022, the traditional Chinese tea making techniques and related customs were successfully included in the *Representative List of Intangible Cultural Heritage of Humanity*, among which Qimen Black Tea making techniques were successfully selected. Traditional Qimen Black Tea relies on handmade production, and the quality depends on the craftsmanship. Therefore, Qimen Blake Tea production technology is also known as "Qimen Kongfu". The production techniques can be divided into two parts: primary processing and refining. Primary processing involves turning fresh leaves into crude tea, and before processing, the fresh leaves are graded to ensure that the raw materials are uniform and

迎客天下
YING KE TIAN XIA

火、匀堆等工序。由此制成的祁门红茶色泽乌润，条索紧细，锋尖秀丽，冲泡时汤色红艳透明，叶底鲜红明亮。其清香持久、独树一帜，被誉为"祁门香"。

黄山茶打开新方式

以前，一套茶具、一盏香茗，就可以细细品味茶中各种滋味。如今，一杯饮品，有花香、茶香抑或是咖啡香，这是新式茶饮年轻人喜爱的方式。在黄山，小小的一片茶叶正碰撞出舌尖上的多种可能。

今年春茶上新之际，黄山毛峰与瑞幸咖啡跨界打造 CP 活动，推出了春日限定新品——黄山毛峰拿铁，茶韵与咖啡香相融合，一时间成了流行在饮品界的新宠。后续很多的黄山茶"组 CP 创新行动"给消费群体带来了意料之外的味蕾和身心体验。

在黄山市屯溪区的一家新中式茶馆，店员小孔用雪克杯和捣汁棒将新鲜的芭乐捣成果泥，再将果泥和萃取的太平猴魁茶汁进行搭配，制成了新中式茶饮——"上春山"。"我们基于本土优质茶做出的创新茶饮，既好看又健康，很受年轻人的欢迎。"

在茶馆的点单机上，除了时下流行的围炉煮茶、围榻冰茶，以黄山本土三大名茶为基底的创新茶饮名列消费榜单前几名。"遇见黄山、黄山云海、水墨徽州、青黛仙露……这些创新茶饮，有的添了酒酿，有的加了茶冻，还有的佐以芝麻糊。通过自己的尝试才知道，

prevent the mixture of old and tender leaves, as well as inferior and impurities. Primary processing includes withering, rolling, fermentation, drying, and others. The initial tea leaves are called crude tea and must be refined before becoming commercial tea. The purpose of refining is to adjust the shape, classify grades, remove impurities, reduce moisture, shrink the volume, so as to facilitate packaging and storage, and meet the specifications of standard tea samples at all levels. Refining includes processes such as screening, cutting, air selection, picking, blending, reheating, and uniform stacking. The Qimen Black Tea after this procedure has black color with luster in tight and fine shape with beautiful sharp edges, and a bright red and transparent soup color when brewed, with bright red leaves at the bottom. The long lasting fragrance is known as the "Qimen fragrance".

New Ways to Enjoy Huangshan Tea

In the past, with a set of tea utensils and a cup of fragrant tea, one could savor the various flavors of tea. Nowadays, a cup of tea with floral, tea, or coffee aromas is a popular way for young people to enjoy modern tea drinks. In Huangshan, a small piece of tea is colliding with various possibilities on the tip of the tongue.

This spring, Mount Huangshan Maofeng teamed up with Luckin Coffee to create a cross-industry event, and launched a spring season limited product—Mount Huangshan Maofeng Latte, which combines the fragrance of tea and coffee, becoming a new favorite beverage overnight. Many

原来茶可以组合这么多材料。"来自上海的年轻情侣说。

"食"徽系美味 "宿"徽州美宿

谈起徽州，总会联想到青砖白瓦、烟雨朦胧；体验徽州，从最具烟火气的徽州美食和徽州民宿开始。

徽菜臭鳜鱼

徽菜，中国八大菜系之一。徽菜以徽州地方菜肴为代表，以徽州特产为主要原料，以民间传统烹调技法为基础。其主要风味特点为咸鲜为主，突出本味，讲究火功，注重食补。其中，徽菜臭鳜鱼是一绝。

两百多年前，徽商在运输上要耗费很长时间，怕随身带的鲜鱼变质，便在桶内撒上盐并在路上经常翻动，阴差阳错造就了特殊风味。今天，臭鳜鱼因独特的制作方法使它散发出一种奇臭的异香气味，俘获着现代人的味蕾。来黄山游玩的一位马来西亚游客说，"它的肉还蛮滑的，口味不错，味道可以接受。以前没有吃过这种鱼，闻起来臭，但是吃起来还挺香的"。

过去以传统方式加工制作的臭鳜鱼往往口味偏咸、肉质偏硬、臭味不稳定。为解决这些问题，人们改良了传统的制作工艺，从取材把关、优化配料调配、精确腌制、冷链运输存储等环节，通过设备的标准化流水作业，达到鲜嫩爽口、臭味稳定的品质。

subsequent "pairing innovation actions" of Huangshan tea have brought unexpected gustatory and sensory experiences to consumer groups.

In a new Chinese teahouse in Tunxi District, Huangshan City, the clerk Xiao Kong made a new Chinese tea drink-Climbing Spring Mountain by pounding fresh guava into fruit puree with a shaker cup and a stick, and then matching the fruit puree with the extracted Taiping Houkui tea. "Our innovative tea drink, based on high-quality local tea, is both visually appealing and healthy, and very popular among young people."

On the menu of the teahouse, in addition to the currently popular "Roast Tea by the Fire" and "Ice Tea by the Sofa", the innovative tea drinks based on the three famous local teas in Huangshan ranks top in the consumption list. "Meet Mount Huangshan, Mount Huangshan Cloud Sea, Huizhou in Ink Painting, Qingdai Xianlu... among these innovative tea drinks, some add wine, some add tea jelly, and some add sesame paste. Through my own attempts, I knew that tea could combine so many materials," said a young couple from Shanghai.

Taste Huizhou Cuisine and Live in Huizhou Mansion

When talking about Huizhou, one can't help but associate it with the traditional architecture of black bricks

迎客天下
YING KE TIAN XIA

"深渡是徽州歙县的一个古码头，明清时徽商来往于徽州与浙江做生意，每每离家时要背上包袱，返家后要卸下包袱，深渡的饮食摊主遂仿其形，创制出一种在馄饨皮上放馅，卷包成如商人背负的包袱形状的小吃，这就是深渡包袱饺的由来。"在某平台直播间内，穿着徽娘服的工作人员正热情地向观众讲述美食背后的故事。这样的场景，在互联网电商平台无数次上演着，一遍遍将徽州的饮食文化传递出去，让美食不仅仅是美食。

在很长一段时间内，臭鳜鱼只流传于长三角一带。如今，它插上电商腾飞的翅膀，发展势头强劲，吸引了更多的消费者。随着臭鳜鱼被越来越多的食客所熟知，徽州美食在纪录片、社交媒体上频频亮相，年产值不断创新高。

徽州民宿

黄山不仅有徽州美食，还有徽州民宿。徽州民宿是烟雨徽州、村落徽州、田园徽州的缩影，沿袭着徽派建筑特色，寄托着故土依恋，抚慰着游子心灵，西溪南村是典型代表之一。

黄山市徽州区丰乐河岸的西溪南村似一幅流动的山水画，小桥流水，鸟语花香，镶嵌的石板路，横跨小溪的古桥，参天的老树，粉墙黛瓦的古民居错落掩映在绿荫后。烟雨徽州枫杨林里的村落让人感受到不

and white tiles, and the misty rain. To experience Huizhou, one can start with the most authentic Huizhou cuisine and accommodations.

Stinky Mandarin Fish

Anhui cuisine is one of the eight major cuisines in China. Anhui cuisine is represented by Huizhou local dishes, with Huizhou specialties as the main raw materials, and traditional folk cooking techniques as the basis. Its main flavor characteristics are salty and fresh, highlighting the original flavor, emphasizing fire skills, and focusing on food tonic. Among them, Anhui cuisine stinky mandarin fish is a unique dish.

More than 200 years ago, Huizhou merchants spent a long time on transportation, worrying that the fresh fish they carried with them would spoil. They sprinkled salt in barrels and frequently tossed them during the trip, creating a special flavor by chance. Today, the stinky mandarin fish emits a strange and pungent odor due to its unique production method, capturing the taste buds of modern people. A Malaysian tourist visiting Mount Huangshan said, "The fish is quite slippery and tastes good, and the taste is acceptable. I haven't eaten this fish before, and it smells bad but tastes delicious."

The traditional production process for stinky mandarin fish used to have a salty taste, tough texture, and unstable smell. To solve these problems, the process has been improved. From selecting raw materials, optimizing ingredient blending, precise marinating, to cold chain

迎客天下
YING KE TIAN XIA

一样的烟火气和生命力。在村落里沿着长长的石板桥走，石板桥尽头右拐就到了著名的枫杨林湿地。多次踏访西溪南的上海游客告诉我们："夏天西溪南的枫杨林最具有生命力！"

进入村落，走在板桥路上，小村巷里，有把番茄装进筐篓贩卖的菜农，也有在自家门口用小板凳、油漆桶、石头当作摊位的小贩，摊位错落有致地排在小巷里。走近观察可以发现，摆摊位的大都是老人。他们把自己家菜园里面种的蔬菜，比如番茄、干笋、梅干菜，拿到摊位上贩卖给游客。村民吴女士介绍说："在旅游旺季的时候，只卖新鲜的笋一天最高就能卖出200元。"

西溪南古村落地处黄山市腹地，背山面水。近年来随着旅游业民宿的开发，古村落迎来了新篇章。西溪南古村落的民宿分为两种：一种是原宿，主要是村民们把自己闲置出来的杂物间、柴房进行改造，摇身一变成为别具一格的民宿。他们用心装饰，保留了乡土风情的同时融入了现代化元素，让游客体验乡村生活，亲近自然。另一种是创意民宿，主要由外来投资者经营，更加注重个性化设计与创新元素的融入。其中原宿占古村落的1/3，创意民宿占比2/3。在民宿的建设过程中，民宿的卫生打扫、厨师、清洁工等岗位招人，村里清闲的老人去应聘，由此从村里默默无闻

transportation and storage, the process is standardized through automated production lines, resulting in a fresh and delicate taste with consistent pungent flavor.

"Shendu is an ancient dock in Shexian County. In the Ming and Qing dynasties, Huizhou merchants were traveling between Huizhou and Zhejiang to do business. They always carried their baggage when they left home, and then they unloaded it when they returned home. The food stall owners in Shendu imitated its shape and created a snack with stuffing on the Wonton skin and rolled it into the shape of a baggage carried by businessmen. This is the origin of Shendu Baofu Dumplings." In a live broadcast room on a platform, the staff in Huiniang clothes were enthusiastically telling the story about the food to the audience. Such scenes have been staged countless times on the Internet e-commerce platform, transmitting Huizhou's food culture over and over again, making food more than just food.

For a long time, stinky mandarin fish was only popular in the Yangtze River Delta. Nowadays, with the wings of e-commerce soaring, the development momentum is strong, attracting more consumers. With the increasing popularity of stinky mandarin fish among diners, Huizhou cuisine has continuously reached new highs in annual output value through frequent appearances in documentaries and on social media.

Huizhou Homestay

Huangshan City has not only Huizhou cuisine, but also Huizhou homestay. Huizhou homestay is a microcosm

迎客天下
YING KE TIAN XIA

西溪南板桥路（程向阳　摄）

Banqiao Road in Xixinan Village (Photo by Cheng Xiangyang)

的老者成为民宿不可或缺的一部分。他们与游客谈论西溪南古村落的故事，成为古村落文化的传递者。

　　黄山的许多民宿，就在这些古村落古建筑的基础上翻新改造。通过"古村落＋新民宿"融合发展，古韵与气韵同台，既保持了"粉墙黛瓦马头墙、回廊挂

of misty rain, villages and pastoral of Huizhou. It follows the characteristics of Huizhou architecture, embodies the attachment to the homeland, and soothes the hearts of travelers. Xixinan Village is one of the typical representatives.

The Xixinan Village on the bank of Fengle River in Huizhou District, Huangshan City, looks like a flowing landscape painting, with small bridges and flowing water, birds singing and fragrant flowers, inlaid stone roads, ancient bridges across streams, towering old trees, and ancient folk houses with white walls and black tiles scattered behind the green shade. The villages in the misty rain of Huizhou and the maple and poplar forests make people feel different flavor of life and vitality. Walking along the long stone bridge in the village, turning right at the end of the bridge leads to the famous Maple and Poplar Forest Wetland. A Shanghai tourist who had visited Xixinan multiple times told us, "In summer, the maple and poplar forests in Xixinan are the most vibrant."

Entering the village, walking on Banqiao Road, in the small village alley, there are vegetable farmers who sell tomatoes in baskets, as well as vendors who use small stools, paint buckets, and stones as stalls at their doorstep. The stalls are arranged in a staggered manner in the alley. When we walked into the booth, we found that most of the people who set up stalls were old people. They sold vegetables grown in their own vegetable garden, such as tomatoes, dried bamboo shoots, and Meigancai, to tourists. Ms. Wu, a villager, introduced that during the peak tourist season, fresh bamboo

迎客天下
YING KE TIAN XIA

落花格窗"的原生模样,又加载了便捷、舒适的现代服务功能。从未晞园、澍德堂、梅姑娘,到黎阳观厅、黄山云亼、拾庭画驿等一批民宿集群的建成运营,形成了一批有特色的民宿集群,徽州民宿品牌影响力将进一步扩大。住徽州民宿逐渐成为一种新时尚,村落

西溪南村(程向阳 摄)

Xixinan Village (Photo by Cheng Xiangyang)

shoots can be sold for up to 200 yuan per day.

Xixinan Village is located in the hinterland of Huangshan City, facing water and behind the mountain. In recent years, with the development of tourism homestays, the ancient village ushers in a new chapter. There are two types of homestays in the ancient Xixinan Village. One is the original homestay, where villagers transform their idle utility rooms and firewood rooms into unique homestays. They decorate them with care, preserving local customs while incorporating modern elements, allowing tourists to experience rural life and get close to nature. Another type is creative homestays, mainly managed by outside investors who pay more attention to the integration of personalized design and innovative elements. Among them, original homestays account for one-third of the ancient village, while creative homestays account for two-thirds. During the construction of homestays, positions such as chef and cleaner were recruited, and the idle elderly in the village applied for them. As a result, they were no longer unknown elders in the village, but became an indispensable part of homestays. They tell tourists the stories of the ancient village in Xixinan, becoming cultural transmitters of the ancient village.

Many homestays in Huangshan City are renovated on the basis of these ancient villages and buildings. Through the integrated development of "ancient villages + new homestays", the ancient charm and atmosphere are on

迎客天下
YING KE TIAN XIA

徽州成为安放心灵的"诗和远方"。

各享其行　畅游徽州

黄山三公里航站跑道可连通世界各大城市，纵横交错的高铁高速交通网络让世界触手可及。

"醉美"公路

"没想到山区公路边居然有这样一个好地方，停车位很充裕，长廊是典型的徽派风格，还建有卫生间开放给大家使用，正好可以让我们在途中休息一下。"一名沿着S218省道旅游风景道自驾旅游途径羊栈岭公路服务点的车友感慨道。

黄山以景区标准推进全路域品质提升，打造更多主客共享、友爱美好的公路新场景，解锁更多出行小美好，更好满足市民和游客的情绪价值。沿着S103省道度假旅游的人渐渐多了起来，路上经常可以看见骑行和自驾的游客。"随着S103省道越建越好，沿线的景区景点也快速发展，我们村年接待游客显著增多，顺势带动了农家乐、民宿和茶叶等农、文、旅消费。"长潭村吴书记说。采用先进的超薄沥青罩面技术对S103省道进行"白改黑"改造，成为安徽省首条超薄沥青公路，让公路出行更安全、更舒适、更静音。同时，在公路沿途打造多个节点，配套建成线路图、观

the same stage, maintaining the original appearance of "white walls, black tiles, horse head walls, and corridors with hanging flower lattice windows", while also adding convenient and comfortable modern service functions. The establishment and operation of a number of homestay clusters, such as Weixi Garden, Shudetang, Meiguniang, Liyang Guanting, Huangshan Yunji, Shiting Huayi, has formed a number of distinctive homestay clusters, and the brand influence of Huizhou homestay will be further expanded. Staying in Huizhou homestays has gradually become a new trend, and the villages of Huizhou has become a "poetry and distant place" for placing the soul.

Enjoy the Journey and Travel Freely in Huizhou

Huangshan has a three-kilometer terminal runway, which can connect major cities in the world. The crossing and intersecting high-speed rail and transportation network makes the world within reach.

The Breathtaking Beauty of the Highway

"I didn't expect there to be such a good place along the mountain road. There are plenty of parking lots, and the long corridor is a typical Huizhou style. There are also bathrooms for everyone to use. It is perfect for us to rest on the way," said a tourist passing by Yangzhanling Highway Service Area, who drove along S218 Provincial Highway Tourist Scenic Road.

迎客天下
YING KE TIAN XIA

景台、停车区等服务设施，在服务中展现黄山公路的友好，让公路出行更便捷、更休闲、更愉悦。

黄山市形成以"米字型"高速公路网为主轴，"叶网"状国省道为支撑，县乡村道为补充的内外联动畅通的公路网布局，把全市乡村连接起来，畅通全域旅游。

高铁枢纽

2024年4月26日，池黄高铁开通，黄山全域进入高铁时代，一跃成为仅次于上海、杭州、南京、合肥的长三角第五大交通枢纽。

8年前，黄山只有一个2台8线的二等小站黄山站。如今，高铁深度改变了这个城市。2015年6月28日，跨越皖赣闽三省、从巢湖之滨抵海峡西岸的合福高铁开通运营，黄山北站正式启用，结束了黄山不通高铁的历史。2018年12月25日，杭昌高铁杭黄段开通运营，黄山北站由5台7线扩展为13台17线，运输能力进一步提升。2023年12月27日，随着杭昌高铁黄昌段的建成通车，杭昌高铁全线贯通，黄山市形成两条高铁动脉的十字形交叉，枢纽地位进一步提升。2024年，黄山西站建成使用，池黄高铁正式通车。不足10年，黄山已从只办理普速旅客乘降业务的旅游城市，一跃成为皖东南高铁枢纽。

"我们有一些同事家住祁门，以往辗转4个小时才

Huangshan City promotes the quality improvement of the whole road area with the standard of scenic spot, creates more new scenes of road for local people and tourists to share better meeting the emotional value of citizens and tourists. More and more people are vacationing and traveling along S103 Provincial Highway, and you can often see tourists cycling and driving along the way. "With the construction of S103 getting better and better, the scenic spots along the route have also developed rapidly. Our village has also received a significant increase in tourists annually, which has driven agricultural, cultural, and tourism consumption such as rural tourism, homestays, and tea," said Secretary Wu of Changtan Village. Adopting advanced ultra-thin asphalt overlay technology to transform S103 "from white to black", it has become the first ultra-thin asphalt highway in Anhui Province, making road travel safer, more comfortable, and quieter. At the same time, a number of nodes will be built along the road, and supporting service facilities, such as road maps, viewing platforms, parking areas, will be built to show the friendliness of Huangshan road, making road traveling more convenient, leisure and pleasant.

Huangshan City has formed an internal and external interconnected and smooth road network layout, with the " 米 " shaped expressway network as the main axis, the leaf-shaped national and provincial highways as the support, and rural roads as the supplement. This network connects all rural areas in the city and facilitates all-around tourism.

迎客天下
YING KE TIAN XIA

黄山高速铁路（樊成柱 摄）
The high-speed railway in Huangshan City (Photo by Fan Chengzhu)

能到达合肥。昌景黄高铁开通后，他们只需一半不到的时间！"一位在合肥上班的市民说。昌景黄高铁通车后，黄山市全面实现联通合肥、杭州、南昌的"两个小时交通圈"，联通上海、武汉、南京、福州等城市的

High-Speed Railway Hub

On April 26, 2024 Chi-Huang high-speed railway was opened, and Huangshan City entered the era of high-speed railway, becoming the fifth largest transportation hub in the Yangtze River Delta after Shanghai, Hangzhou, Nanjing and Hefei.

Eight years ago, Huangshan City had only one second-class station, Huangshan Station, with two sets and eight lines. Nowadays, high-speed railway has profoundly changed this city. On June 28, 2015, the Hefei-Fuzhou high-speed railway, which spans Anhui, Jiangxi and Fujian provinces and extends from the coast of Chaohu Lake to the west coast of the strait, was put into operation, and Huangshan North Station was officially opened, ending the history of lack of high-speed railway in Huangshan. On December 25, 2018, the Hangzhou-Huangshan section of Hangzhou-Nanchang high-speed railway was put into operation, and the Huangshan North Station was expanded from 5 sets and 7 lines to 13 sets and 17 lines, further improving the transportation capacity. On December 27, 2023, with the completion and opening of the Huangzhou-Nanchang section of the Hangzhou-Nanchang high-speed railway, the whole line of the railway will be completed, and Huangshan City forms a crisscross intersection of two high-speed railways, further improving its hub status. In 2024, Huangshan West Station was completed and put into use, and Chizhou-Huangshan high-speed railway was officially opened. Within

迎客天下
YING KE TIAN XIA

"三小时交通圈"。黄山因山立市、以旅兴市。"过去大家提到黄山,只知道是一座山。其实,黄山不仅是一座山,更是一座城,全域处处是景点,步步有文化。"黄山市委书记凌云说。随着黟县东站、祁门南站的开通,黄山的乡村全面打开了,黄山巨大的宝藏和发展潜力让更多人了解了其独特的文化,看到了美丽的风光。美食、美宿、乡村、民俗、非遗等徽式生活,打开了全域旅游的图景。

空中走廊

黄山屯溪国际机场是黄山市的空中门户,是安徽省第二大民用机场。黄山屯溪国际机场开通国内航线20多条,直达北京、广州、深圳等城市;成功开通多条国际航线,直达中国香港、泰国曼谷、新加坡、韩国首尔等国(境)外城市,全力打造大黄山世界级休闲度假康养目的地。

2024年4月19日,中国黄山—泰国曼谷航线正式开通,这是黄山屯溪国际机场新冠疫情转段后恢复的首条国际航线。黄山屯溪国际机场后续将加大境外航班的恢复力度,逐步增开至越南胡志明、河内,菲律宾马尼拉及韩国首尔、釜山等国际航线。

"正如中国游客去法国,一定要爬埃菲尔铁塔一样,我们来到长三角,就绝不能错过大黄山。每次来黄山,我都仿佛走进一幅中国传统山水画。作为多次

less than a decade, Huangshan has transformed from a tourist city that only dealt with boarding and landing of ordinary speed passengers to a high-speed railway hub in Southeast Anhui.

"Some of our colleagues who live in Qimen used to travel for 4 hours to reach Hefei. After the opening of the Nanchang-Jingdezhen-Huangshan high-speed railway, they only need less than half the time," said a citizen working in Hefei. After the opening of Nanchang-Jingdezhen-Huangshan high-speed railway, Huangshan has fully realized the "two hour traffic circle" connecting Hefei, Hangzhou and Nanchang, and the "three hour traffic circle" connecting Shanghai, Wuhan, Nanjing, Fuzhou and other cities. Huangshan is built for the mountain and thrives for tourism. "When people mentioned Huangshan in the past, they only knew that it was a mountain. In fact, Huangshan is not only a mountain, but also a city. The whole region is full of scenic spots and culture," said Ling Yun, secretary of Huangshan Municipal Party Committee. With the opening of Yixian East Railway Station and Qimen South Railway Station, the countryside of Huangshan has been fully opened. The huge treasure and development potential of Huangshan has enabled more people to understand the unique culture and see the beautiful scenery. Delicious food, beautiful accommodations, rural areas, folk customs, intangible cultural heritage and other symbolic lifestyles have opened up the prospect of comprehensive tourism.

迎客天下
YING KE TIAN XIA

黄山屯溪国际机场（程向阳 摄）

Huangshan Tunxi International Airport (Photo by Cheng Xiangyang)

爬过黄山的忠实粉丝，希望有更多国际友人可以来发现黄山的魅力。"一名来自法国的游客说。

　　黄山市的发展要以推进高质量发展为主题，立足文化、生态、区位、旅游等优势，锻长板、补短板、筑底板，刷新黄山形象，重构黄山价值，重塑城市能级，精心描绘中国式现代化的黄山图景。聚力做实特

The Air Corridor

Huangshan Tunxi International Airport is the air portal of Huangshan City and the second largest civil airport in Anhui Province. Huangshan Tunxi International Airport has opened more than 20 domestic routes to Beijing, Guangzhou, Shenzhen and other cities, and has successfully opened a number of international routes to Hong Kong (China), Bangkok (Thailand), Singapore, Seoul (South Korea) and other foreign cities, making every effort to build Grand Huangshan world-class leisure and healthcare destination.

On April 19, 2024, the route from Huangshan, China to Bangkok, Thailand, was officially opened, which is the first international route recovered after the epidemic situation in Huangshan Tunxi International Airport. Huangshan Tunxi International Airport will increase the recovery of overseas flights and gradually open international routes to Ho Chi Minh and Hanoi in Vietnam, Manila in the Philippines, and Seoul and Busan in South Korea.

"Just as Chinese tourists must climb the Eiffel Tower when they go to France, when we come to the Yangtze River Delta, we cannot miss Mount Huangshan. Every time I come to Mount Huangshan, I feel like walking into a traditional Chinese landscape painting. As a loyal fan who has climbed Mount Huangshan many times, I hope that more international friends can come to discover the charm of Mount Huangshan," said a tourist from France.

The development of Huangshan City should take the

迎客天下
YING KE TIAN XIA

色经济，加快发展方式绿色转型，大力发展徽州美食民宿等乡愁经典产业，全面构建与黄山生态环境相适应的现代化产业体系。随着高铁时代的来临，黄山市的交通能级不断提升，承东启西、连南接北的区位优势日益彰显。

promotion of high-quality development as the theme, based on the advantages of culture, ecology, location, tourism and so on, to forge a long board, mend the weak board, build a floor, refresh the image of Mount Huangshan, reconstruct the value of Mount Huangshan, reshape the city's energy level, and carefully depict the Chinese path to modernization of Mount Huangshan. We will work hard to strengthen the featured economy, accelerate the green transformation of the development mode, vigorously develop classic homesickness industries such as Huizhou cuisine and homestay, and comprehensively build a modern industrial system that is compatible with the ecological environment of Mount Huangshan. With the advent of the high-speed railway era, Huangshan City's transportation level has been continuously improved, and the regional advantages of connecting the east to the west and connecting the south to the north are increasingly evident.

和美乡村
宜居宜业

  黄山市现辖7个区县，101个乡镇，689个行政村。全市拥有490余处国家、省级传统村落。多年来，黄山市加快农村一二三产融合发展，创新实施党建带群建促乡村振兴满天星工程；走好绿色发展之路，全域推广"五微"行动，勾勒出烟雨徽州、田园徽州、村落徽州的新图景；深入开展党建引领信用村建设，以法治定分止争，以德治春风化雨，以自治消解矛盾，让黄山乡村既充满活力又和谐有序。宜居宜业和美乡村从一个点的风韵到一条线的风光，连成面上的风景，焕发出无限生机和活力。

6

Livable and Business-Friendly, Harmonious and Beautiful Countryside

Huangshan City is currently divided into 7 districts (counties), with 101 towns and 689 administrative villages. The city has over 490 national and provincial traditional villages. For many years, Huangshan City has been accelerating the integration of the first, second, and third industries in rural areas, innovatively implementing the Starry Sky Project in which Party building leads group building to promote rural revitalization; taking the path of green development, and promoting the "Five Micro" action in the full region, which has depicted a new landscape of the misty rain in Huizhou, the countryside in Huizhou, and the villages in Huizhou; Huangshan has deeply carried out the Party-led credit village construction, using the rule of law to settle disputes, using moral governance to nourish the hearts and minds of the people, using self-governance to resolve conflicts, so that Huangshan's rural areas are both vibrant and harmonious. Livable, business-friendly, harmonious and beautiful rural areas exude boundless vitality and energy, from the charm of a single point to the scenery along a line, which connects to form a landscape on the surface.

迎客天下
YING KE TIAN XIA

共同富裕惠村民

山岔村

山岔村位于黄山风景区东南麓汤口镇，属黄山风景区的一部分，离黄山风景区仅5公里，205国道、103省道横穿而过。全村13个村民组，人口2500余人。

山岔村（程向阳　摄）

Shancha Village (Photo by Cheng Xiangyang)

Common Prosperity Benefits Villagers

Shancha Village

Shancha Village is located in the southeast foot of the Mount Huangshan Scenic Area, Tangkou Town, which is a part of the Mount Huangshan Scenic Area. It is only 5 kilometers away from the scenic area. G205 National Highway and S103 Provincial Highway cross through the village. There are 13 villager groups with a population of over 2,500. The village Party branch committee has 4 subordinate branches, with over 100 Party members. Tourism is the village's leading industry, with 4 tourist attractions, including 2 4A-level scenic spots, 2 rural tourism reception points, and a total of nearly 2,000 guest beds. More than 75% of the village's labor force are engaged in the tourism industry.

In 1987, the villagers of Shangzhang Group, Shancha Village, who were living near a gold mine but leading a poor life, seized the opportunity and invested 1,436 acres of mountain fields to develop the Jade Valley scenic area, registering the first tourism company in China to be operated and managed by farmers. They thus pioneered the development of tourism by farmers nationwide. They have successively developed Jiulong Waterfall, Fenghuangyuan and other 5 natural ecological scenic spots, and the tourism industry has developed from a single "dot" to the whole village "blossoming". In 1999, the villagers of Shangzhang Group made room for idle houses and started the

迎客天下
YING KE TIAN XIA

村党总支下辖4个党支部，共有党员100多名。旅游业为村龙头产业，拥有景区4处，其中国家4A级景区2个，农家乐接待点2处，总接待床位近2000张，旅游从业人员占全村劳动力的75%以上。

1987年，守着金山过着穷日子的山岔村上张组村民抢抓先机，以1436亩山场入股开发了翡翠谷景区，正式注册中国第一家由农民经营管理的黄山翡翠谷旅游公司，开创了全国农民办旅游的先河。先后开发了九龙瀑、凤凰源等5个自然生态景区，旅游业由一个村民组"点上结果"到整村"面上开花"。1999年，上张组村民腾出闲置房屋，率先开启农家乐旅游，成立翡翠人家农家乐旅游有限公司，与农户签订住房合作协议，依托景区发展特色民宿，引导农民走"生态旅游＋共同富裕"之路。2003年建设翡翠新村，2015年左右民宿兴起，瀑布咖啡、丛林穿越等新业态的开发，山岔村旅游经过了景区开发、发展农家乐到精品民宿的升级提升，从单一的看山玩水到休闲度假康养综合型旅游。

山岔村在"做大蛋糕"的同时"分好蛋糕"，探索"四次分配"共富机制，书写共同富裕的传奇故事。通过股份制改革，将13个村民组作为最小集体经济组织单元入股到旅游公司，完成组织运营模式，形成共同富裕的利益联结机制。首次工资分配，18～60周岁

rural tourism business, establishing the Jade Household Farm Tourism Co., Ltd. They signed housing cooperation agreements with farmers and relied on scenic spots to develop characteristic inns, guiding farmers to take the path of "ecological tourism + common prosperity". In 2003, the Jade new village was built, and the rise of homestay was in 2015. At present, with the development of new business forms such as waterfall coffee and jungle crossing, Shancha Village tourism has gone through the development of scenic spots, the development of rural music, to the upgrading of boutique homestay, from simple scenic tour to comprehensive tourism.

Shancha Village has been exploring a shared prosperity mechanism of "distributing the cake fairly" while "making the cake bigger" and writing a legendary story of common prosperity. Through the reform of stock ownership, 13 village groups were incorporated into the tourism company as the smallest unit of collective economic organization, completing the organizational operation model, and forming a mechanism of common prosperity by linking interests. The first salary distribution: 18~60 years old villagers can work in the tourism company, with an average monthly salary of 3,000 yuan. The second redistribution of dividends: based on the annual tourism revenue, the village shareholders will share the dividends together, with each villager receiving an annual dividend of about 16,000 yuan. The third welfare distribution: More than 400,000 yuan is invested annually to provide new rural cooperative medical care and new rural pension for all villagers.

迎客天下
YING KE TIAN XIA

村民可在旅游公司上班，人均月工资3000元；二次红利分配，根据年旅游收益，村民股东共享红利，每人每年享受分红约1.6万元；三次福利分配，每年投入40余万元为全村村民缴纳新农合、新农保；四次优待分配，率先创建村组老年公寓，60周岁以上老人入住食宿全免，实施大学生奖励，考取大学奖励1.5万~2万元。

山岔村2015年被评为全国休闲农业与乡村旅游示范点，2017年被评为全国生态文化村，2020年被评为第二批全国乡村旅游重点村。

芦荔村

芦荔村位于祁门县安凌镇，地处县城东北部，素有"祁门粮仓"之称，为历代官家囤粮之地。芦荔村位于国家4A级牯牛降景区山脚下、秋浦河的源头。这里峰高谷低、田平地阔、山环水绕、气候温和，是粮食种植的人间福地，也是祁门粮食核心产区。芦荔村的祖祖辈辈依托这方好山好水、好田好地，世世代代以种粮为主业，积累形成了成熟的水稻种植经验。

前些年，随着农村主要劳动力陆续外出务工，加之种粮周期长、劳动量大、收入低等因素，一些粮田一度出现撂荒现象。为了守稳守住"祁门粮仓"，芦荔村"两委"与驻村工作队多方走访、广纳群言，于2019年8月牵头成立水稻专业合作社，注册"芦荔清

The fourth preferential distribution: the village will create the first village and group elderly nursing home, and elderly people over 60 years old can live and dine there for free. Implement a scholarship program for college students, rewarding those who pass the college entrance exam with 15,000~20,000 yuan.

Shancha Village was named as a National Demonstration Point for Leisure Agriculture and Rural Tourism in 2015, a National Eco-Cultural Village in 2017, and one of the second batch of National Rural Tourism Key Villages in 2020.

Luli Village

Luli Village is located in Anling Town, northeastern Qimeng County, and is known as "Qimeng Granary". It was the place where officials used to store grain. Luli Village is located at the foot of the 4A-level Guniujiang Scenic Area and at the source of Qiupu River, where mountains are high, valleys are low, and fields are flat and wide. Mountains surround it and rivers flow through it with mild climate. It is a paradise for grain planting and the core grain production areas of Qimeng County. The ancestors of the villagers have relied on this good mountains, rivers, fields and land for generations, and have passed down the mature rice planting experience from generation to generation.

In recent years, with the main labor force in rural areas leaving to work in cities, coupled with factors such as a long growing cycle for rice, high labor intensity, and low income, some farmland was left uncultivated for a while. In order to maintain and safeguard the "Qimeng Granary", the village's

迎客天下
YING KE TIAN XIA

水田"商标，由此翻开了浓墨重彩做好"芦荔大米"这篇粮食大文章的序篇。芦荔村积极鼓励农户以耕地入股，吸收家庭农场加入合作社，实行产前、产中、产后全过程综合性服务，摸索"五统一分"（统一规划、统一机耕、统一技术、统一品牌、统一销售、分户管

芦荔村（程向阳 摄）
Luli Village (Photo by Cheng Xiangyang)

"two committees" and the work team conducted extensive visits and solicited public opinions. In August 2019, they took the lead in establishing a rice professional cooperative and registered the "Luli Clear Paddy Field" trademark, thus opening the prologue to writing a grand "Luli Rice" story on the topic of food security. Luli Village actively encourages farmers to invest their farmland in the cooperative, and absorbs family farms to join the cooperative, providing comprehensive services throughout the pre-production, production, and post-production process. It has also explored the "five unified and one divided" (unified planning, unified plowing, unified technology, unified brand, unified sales, and separate management) planting model, enriching and improving the grain industry chain and value chain, and gradually formed the "party building + cooperative + large-scale farmers" business model. The "Luli Rice" produced by the cooperative has evenly shaped grains, like pearls and jade, with fragrant, lightly sweet rice that is highly sought after by the market. In 2022, the rice yield reached 160,000 kilograms, with the village's collective economy earning over 1.46 million yuan.

Next, Luli Village will focus on creating a new development path of "1+6+X" (a division of labor and cooperation model centered on Luli Village in Anling Town, radiating to six neighboring villages, and involving large-scale farmers in the surrounding areas), establish a town-wide grain industry alliance, pool resources to build standardized seedling cultivation bases and grain processing enterprises,

迎客天下
YING KE TIAN XIA

理)种植模式,丰富完善粮食产业链、价值链,逐步形成了"党建+合作社+种粮大户"的经营模式。合作社生产的"芦荔大米"米粒均匀、如珠似玉,米饭芳香、清淡微甜,深受市场欢迎。2022年粮食产量16万公斤,村集体经济收入突破146万元。

接下来,芦荔村将致力于打造"1+6+X"发展新路径(在育秧、社会化服务、烘干、加工、销售等环节,以安凌镇芦荔村为核心,辐射周边6个村,并带动周边大户参与的分工合作模式),成立全镇粮食产业联盟,抱团新建育秧标准化基地和粮食加工企业,鼓励更多村和新型经营主体参与,加快推进田耕文化体验区、粮食故事展示区和粮食产后服务参观区"三区"建设,以产业兴旺全面推进乡村振兴,让老百姓种粮更有甜头、有劲头。芦荔村于2018年被评为省级美丽乡村。

宜居宜业美村民

塔川村

黟县宏村镇塔川村被列入第二批中国传统村落名录。深秋时节,塔川盆地山峦叠翠,村口樟树、香榧和枫树五棵参天古树,各有色彩,五彩斑斓,宛如一幅油画。这里是众多画家、摄影家创作的基地,与四

encourage more villages and new types of economic entities to participate, and accelerate the construction of the "three zones" of the rice paddy cultural experience area, the display area of rice stories, and the post-harvest service observation area, so as to promote industrial prosperity across the countryside and enable farmers to derive more benefits from farming, thereby fully promoting rural revitalization. Luli Village was designated as a provincial beautiful village in 2018.

Livable and Business-Friendly Village Benefits Villagers

Tachuan Village

Tachuan Village, Hongcun Town, Yixian County, is one the second batch of traditional Chinese villages. In late autumn, the mountains in the Tachuan basin are covered in green, and the five ancient trees at the entrance to the village, including the cypress, camphor, and maple trees, each with their own colors, become a riot of colors, resembling a painting. It is a base for many painters and photographers, and is listed as one of the four most beautiful autumn viewing spots in China, along with Jiuzhaigou in Sichuan, Kanas in Xinjiang, and Xiangshan in Beijing. The harmonious "organic architecture" that integrates human beings and nature allows the Huizhou architecture to grow naturally, etching historical and cultural memories into it and becoming a century-old classic that carries the spirit

迎客天下
YING KE TIAN XIA

川九寨沟、新疆喀纳斯和北京香山并列为中国最美的四大赏秋之地。人与自然和谐的"有机建筑",让徽派建筑生长在自然中,铭刻住历史和文化的记忆,成为匠心传承的百年经典。这里让李安、张艺谋、陈凯歌等著名导演流连忘返,成为没有屋顶的摄影棚和没有围墙的影视城。中国著名的电影人张震燕创建的宏村御前侍卫·塔川艺术精品酒店坐落于此。酒店由8幢独立的徽派建筑组成,建筑体为160多年前山村古民居,酒店配备星级酒店硬件设施及贴心的管家式服务。这里已成为创作灵感地、心灵休憩地。

宜居兴村、宜业富民。塔川秋色引游人纷至沓来,也给村民带来了好日子。"景村共生"生态产品价值实现路径正在形成。近年来,塔川村以农为景,加强对水系文脉、田园特色、山体河道、故居老宅、古树古木等乡村风貌的保护和利用,通过农房改造、村庄提升、彩叶树种补植等,留住乡愁记忆。依托独特的风景风貌和村落民居,借力毗邻世界文化遗产地宏村景区所带来的强大客流,引进专业团队,打造特色民宿集群,错位配套发展,带动村中农户经营民宿产业,72家民宿吸纳300余人就业,年经营性收入近3000万元,其中塔川书院于2021年被评定为全国首批甲级旅游民宿。村集体经济由2015年的10.9万元增至2022年的57万元。村民魏涛笑言,"租赁闲置老屋,变成

of craftsmanship. Here, famous directors such as Ang Lee, Zhang Yimou, and Chen Kaige have been enchanted and made it a film set without a roof and a film city. Hongcun Yuqianshiwei · Tachuan Artistic Boutique Hotel, created by China's renowned filmmaker Zhang Zhenyan, is located here. The hotel consists of 8 independent Huizhou-style buildings that were originally ancient rural dwellings over 160 years ago. The hotel is equipped with star-class hotel facilities and provides thoughtful butler-style service, making it a creative inspiration hub and a place for rest and relaxation of the soul.

Liveable communities make villages thriving, and business-friendly enriches people. Tachuan Autumn Colors View attracts tourists in droves, and it also brings good days to the villagers. The realization path of the ecological product value of "scenery and village symbiosis" is taking shape. In recent years, Tachuan Village has been focusing on protecting and utilizing its rural landscape features such as water systems, farmland, mountains, rivers, ancestral homes, old houses, ancient trees, and ancient woodlands, while integrating agriculture into the scenery. Through the renovation of rural houses, enhancement of the village, and planting of colorful tree species, the village has managed to preserve the memories of its rural life. Leveraging its unique scenic landscape and village architecture, taking advantage of the strong influx of tourists brought by the proximity to the World Cultural Heritage site—Hongcun scenic area, and introducing professional teams, the village has developed a

迎客天下
YING KE TIAN XIA

满足市场需求的度假民宿，租用荒废田地，生产五黑农产品，村民来民宿上班。"有了房屋及土地租金，再加上工资，村民每人年收入近 6 万元。

塔川村于 2013 年被列入第二批中国传统村落名录，2017 年被列为国家森林公园，2020 年被评为第二批全

塔川书院（程向阳　摄）
Tachuan Academy Hotel (Photo by Cheng Xiangyang)

unique cluster of characteristic inns, complementing each other in a differentiated manner, and driving local farmers to operate inns, with 72 inns employing over 300 people and generating nearly 30 million yuan in annual operating income. Among them, Tachuan Academy Hotel was designated as one of the first-class tourism inns in China in 2021. The village collective economy has increased from 109,000 yuan in 2015 to 570,000 yuan in 2022. Wei Tao, a villager, said, "We rent out idle old houses and turn them into vacation homes to meet market demand. We rent out abandoned fields to produce agricultural products, and villagers work at the vacation homes." With rental income from houses and land, plus wages, each villager earns nearly 60,000 yuan per year.

Tachuan Village was listed as one of the second batch of Traditional Chinese Villages in 2013, a National Forest Park in 2017, one of the second batch of National Rural Tourism Key Villages in 2020, and one of the first batch of "Weather and Climate Scenic Spots" in China in 2022.

Zuyuan Village

Zuyuan Village, Xikou Town, Xiuning County, founded in the Song Dynasty, is nestled on the slopes of Chajiaojian Mountain, which stands at an altitude of 685 meters, and is a 1,000-year-old ancient Huizhou village that inherits the traditional style and spatial texture of Huizhou. It is known as "dream home and a village like poem and painting".

In 2015, Pang Huantai, a 70-year-old man from Shanghai, first came to Zuyuan Village and was immediately drawn

迎客天下
YING KE TIAN XIA

国乡村旅游重点村，2022年入选全国首批"天气气候景观观赏地"。

祖源村

休宁县溪口镇祖源村，始建于宋代，偎依在海拔685米的插角尖山腰，是一个承继着徽州传统风貌和空间肌理的千年徽州古村落，有"梦里老家，诗画祖源"之誉。

祖源村（朱荣明　摄）

Zuyuan Village (Photo by Zhu Rongming)

to the environment and ancient houses there. He decided to create a dream village in Zuyuan. In November of that year, Pang Huantai established Huangshan Hongsen Investment and Development Co., Ltd. and organized professionals to carry out a comprehensive planning for the village. Based on preserving the traditional style and historical heritage of the village, comprehensive integration of mountain, water, fields, forests, and lakes, etc. has been carried out, with 30 ancient dwellings renovated and 55 guest rooms completed. Modern living experiences have been incorporated into the construction, with one courtyard per building and one model per building, integrating elements such as bookstores, tea bars, bars, coffee shops, and bakeries into the countryside. Classical and fashionable elements are blended together to create the "Zuyuan in the dream" guesthouse cluster, and the village has gradually become known under the leadership of Pang Huantai.

Zuyuan Village Party organization uses grid management, relying on the rural tourism association and the "Rural Tourism Party Building Alliance" brand, to guide villagers from being bystanders in rural governance to becoming participants. More than 20 villagers have converted their homes into homestays, forming a complementary development pattern of high, medium, and low-end consumer groups. Currently, the village can accommodate more than 350 tourists, with the highest number of tourists reaching 150,000 in a year, with an average annual income of over 300,000 yuan per household. A brand new and vibrant

迎客天下
YING KE TIAN XIA

2015年上海花甲老人庞焕泰首次来到祖源村，就被这里的环境和古民房所吸引，毅然决定在祖源打造一个梦里乡村。当年11月，庞焕泰成立黄山宏森投资发展公司，组织专业人士对村庄进行整体规划。在保持古村风貌、历史文脉的基础上，全面整合山、水、田、林、湖等优质资源，改造古民居30栋，完成客房配套55间。在建设中植入现代生活体验场景，按照一栋一庭院、一幢一模式，把书吧、茶吧、酒吧、咖啡屋、面包房等元素融入乡村，将古典与时尚结合，打造"梦里祖源"民宿群，在庞焕泰的带动下，村庄渐渐被人熟知。

祖源村党组织运用网格化管理，依托农家乐协会及"民宿党建联盟"品牌等，引导村民从乡村治理的"旁观者"成为"当事人"。20余户村民将自家房屋改造成农家乐，形成高、中、低层次消费群体互补的发展态势。目前全村接待游客床位达到350多个，年接待游客最高峰达到了15万人次，户年均收入达30万元。一个崭新的、充满活力的祖源村展现在世人面前。

如今的祖源，黄墙黑瓦，曲径通幽，花木扶疏，四季如画。村里建起了黄山市首家村史馆，举办油菜花节、民俗文化节，培育水口思源、长岭思贤等"祖源十景"微景点，挖掘思贤岭等传说和打糍粑等民俗，开通祖源至高山村的登山古道，引进古法油榨作坊文

Zuyuan Village is now presented to the world.

Zuyuan, with its yellow walls and black tiles, winding paths, lush greenery, and scenic views, is now a picturesque village with four distinct seasons. The village has built the first village museum in Huangshan City, hosts an annual rape flower festival and folk culture festival, and has cultivated the micro-scenic spots of "Zuyuan Ten Scenic Spots", including Shuikou Siyuan and Changling Sixian. It has also dug up legends and folklore, such as the legend of Sixian Hill, and making glutinous rice cakes. It has opened a hiking trail from Zuyuan to Gaoshan Village, introduced an ancient oil pressing workshop cultural tourism project, and developed creative study tours and folk tours. Based on the rural scenery, the village adopted the "professional cooperative + farmers + N" development model to lease over 100 mu of Gaowu terraces and abandoned tea gardens, and transformed them into organic fruit gardens to develop village collective economy. By promoting it through TikTok and WeChat, the village actively created the "Dream Village" Zuyuan IP and developed rural tourism businesses such as leisure agriculture, inns and customs, health and wellness, and photography and painting. Suddenly, tourists flocked in, customers filled the village, and the "Dream Village" brand spread across the country. "Visit the Dream Village, taste the flavors of hometown" became popular, and the 1,000-year-old village came to life with boundless vitality.

Zuyuan Village was listed as one of the third batch of China's Traditional Villages in 2014, awarded the title of

化旅游项目，发展创意研学游、民俗游。依托田园风光，按照"专业合作社＋农户＋N"发展模式，流转百亩高坞梯田、荒茶园，打造有机果园，发展村集体经济。通过抖音推介、微信宣传等方式，积极打造"梦乡村"祖源IP，构建休闲农业、民宿民俗、健康养生、摄影写生等乡村旅游业态。一时游人如织，顾客盈门，"梦乡村"品牌飞向全国各地，"游梦里祖源、品老家味道"深入人心，千年古村焕发勃勃生机。

祖源村于2014年被列入第三批中国传统村落名录，2018年被授予全国生态文化村称号，2020年入选第二批全国乡村旅游重点村和中国美丽休闲乡村。

德治善治和村民

大茂社区

大茂社区位于歙县深渡镇西部，是国家地理标志保护产品"三潭枇杷"的主要产区，黄山－千岛湖水上黄金旅游廊道的重要节点。村域总面积9.2平方公里，户籍人口581户、1457人。近年来，大茂深入推进抓党建促乡村振兴，在产业富民、信用治理、人才兴村等方面探索形成了共建共治共享的"大茂样本"。

在村"两委"的带动下，大茂一路探寻创富带富

National Eco-Cultural Village in 2018, and selected as one of the second batch of National Rural Tourism Key Village and China's Beautiful Leisure Countryside in 2020.

Good Governance Through Moral Means Makes Villagers Harmonious

Damao Community

Damao Community is located in the west of Shendu Town, Shexian County, and is the main production area of the national geographical indication protection product Santan Loquat. It is also an important node of the Huangshan-Qiandao Lake waterway golden tourist corridor. The village has a total area of 9.2 square kilometers, with a registered population of 581 households and 1,457 people. In recent years, Damao has deeply promoted the Party building to promote rural revitalization, exploring and forming a shared governance model in the areas of industrial prosperity, credit governance, and talent revitalization.

Under the leadership of the village's "two committees", Damao has been exploring a path to create wealth and bring prosperity to its people. It has actively promoted the cultivation of loquat and tea, established loquat, wood and bamboo processing factories, and opened homestays, all of which have led to a tenfold increase in the income of local people in just ten years.

In 2019, Damao Community seized the opportunity

迎客天下
YING KE TIAN XIA

产业之路，先后大力推广枇杷、茶叶种植，创办枇杷、木竹加工厂及民宿农家乐，让老百姓收入10年增加了10倍。

2019年，大茂社区抓住机遇成功列入全省第一批党建引领信用村建设选点村，深入开展信用评级，引领乡风文明。评出信用主体291家，村集体授信3000

大茂社区（程向阳 摄）
Damao Community (Photo by Cheng Xiangyang)

to successfully become one of the first selected villages for Party-led credit village construction in the whole province, and carried out in-depth credit rating to lead the rural civilization. A total of 291 credit entities were selected, with a credit line of 30 million yuan granted to village collectives and a combined credit line of 28 million yuan granted to credit users, thus turning information into credit and credit into gold. In order to increase the value of integrity, those who are virtuous will have gains. Not only are credit ratings linked to 10 privilege policies, such as medical care, but a credit supermarket has also been established, where villagers can earn points for participating in environmental governance and exchange goods with those points. The construction of the credit system has stimulated new vitality in environmental governance, and every small thing that protects the environment has become a daily routine for every villager. A good atmosphere has been created where those who keep their promises benefit from everything and those who lose their credibility are restricted in all aspects.

Developing grassroots democracy is the vital source of energy for achieving good governance in rural areas. Besides strictly implementing the "four discussions and two public announcements" system, Damao has also innovatively introduced the Householder Meeting and the practice of having village representatives attend Party branch meetings, allowing everyone to be a speaker. Land expropriation, environmental improvement, and project construction are

万元、信用户合计授信 2800 万元，实现了信息变信用、信用变真金。为了让诚信增"值"，德者有"得"，不仅将信用评级和医疗等与政策挂钩，还建立起信用好超市，村民参与环境治理可获得积分兑换物资。信用体系建设激发了环境治理的新活力，守护环境的每一件小事成了每一位村民的日常事，营造了守信事事受益、失信处处受限的良好氛围。

发展基层民主，是实现乡村善治的活力源泉。大茂除了严格落实"四议两公开"等制度，还创新推行户主会、村民代表列席党员大会，让人人都当发言人，田地征用、环境整治、项目建设往往是矛盾比较集中的领域，村民们常常"面红耳赤"开会，"握手言欢"散会。朱家坞枇杷园进园道路项目征地涉及 40 多户，班子成员逐户上门做工作，最终户主会上大家把涉及的 4 亩多地全部无偿捐出，项目既省了钱又省了力。针对邻里间的疑难纠纷，村里建起了综治调解室、徽州乡风评理堂，联合政法部门组建生态公益诉讼检察室、无诉讼社区服务站，用好当地的深渡人民法庭，推行"退一步想"工作法，引导大家换位思考、慎争戒诉，近年成功化解纠纷 200 余起。镇老政法委书记说，"有事村里商量就能解决，政法部门也在家门口，群众没必要上访！"

大茂社区于 2017 年被评为全国创建无邪教示范社

often the topics full of contradictions, and villagers often hold heated meetings, only to "shake hands in friendship" afterward. The land acquisition project for the entrance road to Zhujiawu Loquat Garden involves more than 40 households. The leadership team went door-to-door to do the work, and in the end, the landowners agreed to donate more than 4 acres of land without compensation. The project saved both money and effort. In response to difficult and complicated disputes among neighbors, the village has established a comprehensive governance mediation room, a Huizhou customs mediation hall, and jointly formed an ecological public interest litigation prosecution office and a no-lawsuit community service station. It has also made good use of the Shendu People's Court and promoted the "taking a back step" work method, guiding people to consider each other's perspectives and avoid disputes and lawsuits. In recent years, it has successfully resolved over 200 disputes in this way. The former secretary of the Party's committee for public security said, "If there's a problem, we can solve it by discussing it at the village level. The judicial organs are also right here at our doorstep. There's no need for people to go on a petitioning trip."

Damao Community was named as a National Model Community for Anti-Cult Work in 2017, a China's Characteristic Village in 2020, and a National Democracy and Rule of Law Model Community in 2023.

Zhishan Village

Zhishan Village, also known as Lu Village, is located

迎客天下
YING KE TIAN XIA

区，2020 年被评为中国村庄特色村，2023 年被评为全国民主法治示范社区。

雉山村

雉山村又名卢村，地处黟县北部，毗邻世界文化遗产地宏村，是以卢姓为主聚居的古村落。溪水潺潺、风景秀丽，村中房屋夹溪而建，粉墙黛瓦、小桥流水、炊烟袅袅，宛若现实版《千里江山图》。雉山村始建于南唐时期，至今已有1000多年的历史。卢村文风昌盛，

雉山村（程向阳 摄）
Zhishan Village (Photo by Cheng Xiangyang)

in the northern part of Yixian County and is adjacent to the World Cultural Heritage site—Hongcun. It is an ancient village where the Lu family live in a compact community. The stream flows gently, and the scenery is beautiful. The houses in the village are built along the creek with white walls and black tiles, small bridges, and rising smoke. It feels like a real-life version of the *Thousand Mile River and Mountain Scroll*. Built during the Southern Tang Dynasty, it has a history of over 1,000 years. The culture of learning is flourishing in Lu Village, and the traditional family rules and regulations have been passed down from generation to generation and from mouth to mouth. The ancestors of the Lu family also expressed the essence of these rules and regulations in paintings, couplets, carvings, and hangings in the houses, so that the Lu family descendants could see and hear them every day, and thus regulate their behavior and conduct.

Preserving Huizhou culture and cultivating rural civilization, Zhishan Village has refined and deepened the Lu Village Family Code, which has been passed down for over a thousand years, into a concise and easy-to-understand 90-character "New Three Principles of Zhishan Village"—Good family customs, reading more books; beautiful Zhishan needs everyone to builds; poor people are not greedy, rich people are not arrogant; human nature is good, rural customs are pure... The "New Three Principles of Zhisha Village" has become a village regulation and code of conduct that

迎客天下
YING KE TIAN XIA

传统家训族规代代口传,卢氏祖先还将其精髓要义寓意在画中,寄语予楹联,雕刻在屋内,悬挂于大堂,让卢氏子孙日日耳闻目睹,规范言行。

传承徽州文化,厚植乡风文明,雉山村将千年的卢村家训反复打磨深化,最终精简成通俗易懂、朗朗上口的90字"雉山村新三风"——"家风良、勤读书、雉山美、大家建、贫不馋、富不骄、人性善、民风淳……","雉山村新三风"已成为村中家家户户、田间人人传唱的村规民约,并成为村民日常生活中的尺子,成为乡村自治的行为规范和约束准则。新理念深深植根于村民心中,也让传统乡风文化活了起来。

"村民再也不用撑面子大摆酒席了,既省心又省钱。"为杜绝大吃大喝、大操大办的不良风气,村党组织制定《红白喜事十二条》,帮助村民处理红白喜事,大力倡导不攀不比、节约简办,办喜事、丧事有了标准,红事新办、白事简办、小事不办的新风尚在雉山村蔚然成风。卢村"好媳妇"方顺梅多年来伺候瘫痪在床的婆婆直到过世,并按照要求做到老人白事一切从简。

活用徽州文化,解析治理密码,描绘山水新韵,乡村之美,美在乡风民风。雉山村积极培育文明乡风,激发乡村振兴内生动力,农民群众的获得感、幸福感、安全感持续增强。虽然这座千年古村历经沧桑,却因

is spread by every person in the fields, and has become a yardstick in daily life for villagers. It has also become a behavioral norm and standard of restraint for rural self-governance. The new concept has deeply rooted itself in the hearts of villagers and has brought traditional rural folk culture back to life.

"Villagers are no longer burdened with the need to maintain social appearances through extravagant banquets. This approach is both convenient and cost-effective." In order to eradicate the bad custom of excessive eating and drinking and grandiose celebrations, the village Party organization has formulated the "Twelve Rules for Weddings and Funerals", which helps villagers handle weddings and funerals and actively advocates not comparing oneself with others and keeping things simple. With these rules in place, there is now a new trend in ZhiShan Village where weddings and funerals are held in a simple and frugal manner, and small events are not held at all. The "Good Wife" Fang Shunmei has taken care of her bedridden mother-in-law for many years until her death, and she has complied with the request to keep the funeral simple.

Zhishan Village utilizes the culture of Huizhou, decodes governance secrets, and depicts new rhythms of mountains and waters. The beauty of rural areas lies in the local customs and folkways. Zhishan Village actively cultivates civilized rural customs to stimulate the inner driving force of rural revitalization, and the sense of gain, happiness, and security of the farmers has continued to improve. Although this

迎客天下
YING KE TIAN XIA

"古训今用"的治理模式，依然焕发着勃勃的生机和活力。

雉山村于2012年被列入第一批中国传统村落名录，2014年被评为中国历史文化名村，2016年被评为中国美丽乡村，2022年被评为长三角乡村文化传承创新典型村落。

近年来，黄山市充分发挥生态资源优势，以"村村抱团""村企合作""党组织+企业+合作社+村民"等方式强村富民，以"退一步想"与"进一步为"相结合创新乡村治理方式，走出了一条农文旅融合、点线面交织的乡村大景区之路，一个个宜居宜业和美的现代黄山乡村不断涌现出来。

1,000-year-old village has gone through many hardships, it still exudes vitality and vigor due to its "modernizing ancient customs" governance model.

Zhishan Village was listed as one of the first batch of China's Traditional Villages in 2012, designated as a Chinese Historical and Cultural Village in 2014, named as a Beautiful Chinese Village in 2016, and recognized as a Typical Village for Rural Cultural Inheritance and Innovation in the Yangtze River Delta Region in 2022.

In recent years, Huangshan City has effectively utilized its ecological resources advantage and spearheaded rural revitalization through the implementation of models such as "village-village cooperation", "village-enterprise cooperation", and "party organization + enterprise + cooperative + villagers" to enhance village prosperity and elevate living standards. Furthermore, it has pioneered an innovative rural governance approach that combines the "taking a back step" method mindset with "forward-looking" actions, thus paving the way for a comprehensive rural tourism integration strategy characterized by interconnected nodes, pathways, and development areas, resulting in an increasing number of modern Huangshan rural areas that are both sustainable and thriving.

开放高地 迎客天下

　　黄山有着冠绝天下的自然风光、博大精深的文化、无与伦比的生态环境，这使其成为中国文化和中国叙事的典型代表。黄山作为大黄山世界级IP的"核心高地"，作为长三角一体化高质量发展的"南桥头堡"，作为联通中外的最美"国际会客厅"，正以一座开放枢纽之城的姿态，拥抱全国、迈向全球，成为一个奋进包容的开放高地。

7

An Opening-up Highland Greeting the World

Huangshan City has beautiful natural scenery, extensive and profound culture, and excellent ecological environment, which makes it a typical representative of Chinese culture and Chinese narrative. Huangshan, as the "core highland" of the "Grand Huangshan" world-class IP, as the "south bridgehead" of integrated development of the Yangtze River Delta, and as the most beautiful "international meeting room" connecting China and other countries, is embracing the country and moving toward the world as an open hub city, and becoming an enterprising and inclusive open highland.

迎客天下
YING KE TIAN XIA

大黄山世界级休闲度假康养旅游目的地

为推动区域经济高质量发展，更好发挥大黄山地区的优越区位条件和独特资源禀赋优势，经过两年多的深入谋划，安徽决定建设大黄山世界级休闲度假康养旅游目的地。大黄山囊括了黄山、宣城、池州、安庆4个地级市，共28个县，是跨区域整体联动发展的超级IP。

山水人文冠天下

大黄山山水冠绝天下。黄山、九华山、天柱山、齐云山群峰伫立。黄山是全球首个集世界自然文化"双遗产"、世界地质公园、世界生物圈保护区于一身的自然保护地"全冠王"，天柱山被誉为"最美花岗岩地貌"。区域内水网密布，长江、新安江、秋浦河、青弋江川流不息，太平湖、花亭湖、升金湖、平天湖等湖泊星罗棋布。

大黄山历史人文底蕴深厚。区域内的徽州文化历久弥新，如新安理学主张的"正其义不谋其利，明其道不计其功"，是吸引第三次阿富汗邻国外长会等重大外交活动来此举办的重要人文价值；九华山是佛教四大名山之一，齐云山是道教四大名山之一；安庆薛家岗遗址是新石器时代文化典型代表。黄山文化、徽州

The Grand Huangshan World-Class Leisure and Healthcare Tourism Destination

In order to promote the high-quality development of regional economy and give better play to the superior location conditions and resource endowment advantages of the "Grand Huangshan" region, after more than two years of in-depth planning, Anhui decided to build the Grand Huangshan world-class leisure and healthcare tourism destination. The "Grand Huangshan" includes 4 cities (Huangshan, Xuancheng, Chizhou, Anqing), a total of 28 counties, is the super IP of the cross-regional linkage development.

Renowned for the Landscape and Humanity

Mountains and rivers in the "Grand Huangshan" region are beautiful. Mount Huangshan, Mount Jiuhua, Mount Tianzhu and Mount Qiyun stand on their peaks. Huangshan is a natural and cultural heritage, a world geopark and a world biosphere reserve. Mount Tianzhu is known as "the most beautiful granite landform". The area is densely networked with water. The Yangtze River, Xin'an River, Qiupu River and Qingyi River flow continuously. Taiping Lake, Huating Lake, Shengjin Lake, Pingtian Lake and other lakes are scattered.

The "Grand Huangshan" has profound historical and cultural heritage. The Huizhou culture in the region is enduring and fresh. For example, Xin'an Neo-confucianism advocates

迎客天下
YING KE TIAN XIA

文化、古皖文化、桐城文化、红色文化、诗歌文化等交融发展，文房四宝的发展使哲学、医学、绘画、建筑等各种流派交相辉映。

大黄山的高速公路密度为356公里每万平方公里，连接了区内所有市、县和主要景点。高速铁路网布局得到进一步的提升和完善，区域内4个市同时拥有8条高铁线。黄山机场、九华山机场、芜宣机场、安庆机场等航线联通全国主要城市。畅通的交通实现了与长三角、京津冀、粤港澳主要城市的快速通行。大黄山发达的交通将区域内如此丰富的世界级资源连接在一起，呈现给全世界。

文旅融合新黄山

作为大黄山"核心高地"的黄山市既有深厚的自然和文化资源，又有无比浓厚的生活气息，并注重将得天独厚的资源禀赋与运动休闲、音乐、旅居等现代元素深度融合，催生出黄山特色的文体活动、美食、民宿、度假区……黄山市不断推进一体化文旅发展，打造最具魅力的世界级旅游目的地。

2024年3月10日，黄山首届国际"村BA"在徽州区西溪南镇芝篁村开幕，荷兰羊角村代表队与徽州区西溪南村代表队以球会友，在竞技中深化交流。

2024年3月13日，"艺动中国——2024中国黟县宏村、西递国际水彩艺术季"吸引来自俄罗斯、英国、

that "in the process of pursuing justice and morality, there should not be the idea of seeking personal interests, but should focus on the practice of justice and morality, and do not care about personal credit and interests," which is an important cultural value to attract major diplomatic activities such as the third Foreign Ministers' Meeting among the Neighboring Countries of Afghanistan to hold here. Mount Jiuhua is one of the four famous Buddhist mountains, and Mount Qiyun is one of the four famous Taoist mountains; Anqing Xuejiagang site is the typical representative of the Neolithic age culture. Huangshan culture, Huizhou culture, ancient Anhui culture, Tongcheng culture, red culture, poetry culture and so on integrate and develop. The development of the four treasures of the study makes philosophy, medicine, painting, architecture and other schools complement each other.

The expressway density of the "Grand Huangshan" is 356 kilometers per 10,000 square kilometers, connecting all cities, counties and major scenic spots in the area. The layout of the high-speed railway network has been further improved, and four cities in the region have eight high-speed rail lines. Huangshan Airport, Jiuhuashan Airport, Wuxuan Airport, Anqing Airport and other air routes are connected to major cities in China. The smooth traffic has realized the rapid passage with the Yangtze River Delta, the Beijing-Tianjin-Hebei Region, major cities of Guangdong, Hong Kong and Macao. The developed transportation of the "Grand Huangshan" connects such rich world-class resources in the

迎客天下
YING KE TIAN XIA

比赛现场（樊成柱　摄）

The scene of a match (Photo by Fan Chengzhu)

以色列、黎巴嫩、智利等8个国家的11位国际艺术家代表和来自中国国内的15位艺术家代表参加。他们通过斑斓的色彩、绝美的线条，展现西递、宏村等地的独特风光。俄罗斯水彩艺术家阿纳斯塔西娅·彼得里亚耶娃说："我很高兴能来到这里，我很高兴能在这么美丽的历史名胜中画画。西递是历史悠久遗产的一部分，我真的很喜欢中国的建筑。"加拿大水彩艺术家吉奈特·罗杰斯说："这是我第一次来到这里，我着迷于

region and presents it to the whole world.

Cultural and Tourism Integration of the New Huangshan

As the core highland of the "Grant Huangshan", Huangshan City has not only profound natural and cultural resources, but also a strong life atmosphere. It pays attention to the deep integration of unique resource endowment with modern elements such as sports, leisure, music, travel and residence, giving birth to the cultural and sports activities, food, homestay and resort areas. Huangshan City continues to promote the development of integrated cultural tourism and creates the most attractive world-class tourism destination.

On March 10, 2024, the first Huangshan international "village basketball game" opened in Zhihuang Village, Xixinan Town, Huizhou District. The representative team of Giethoorn Village and the representative team of Xixinan Village deepen exchanges in the competition.

On March 13, 2024, "Art China — 2024 China Hongcun, Xidi International Watercolor Art Season" attracted 11 international artists from 8 countries, such as Russia, Britain, Israel, Lebanon, Chile and so on, and 15 artists from China to participate. They show the unique scenery of Xidi and Hongcun through colorful colors and beautiful lines. The Russian watercolor artist said, "I am very happy to be here. I am very happy to draw in such a beautiful historical spot. Xidi is a part of the long historical heritage. I really like Chinese architecture." "This is my first time here," said Canadian watercolor artist

它的美丽和古老，我希望永远坐在这里画画。"

百度和黄山联合打造 5 万人春日音乐嘉年华，以非遗传承、科技体验为核心亮点，以民谣、摇滚、嘻哈、流行等不同音乐类型为内容，登上热榜，成为大众关注的焦点。

在这座友好美丽、开放包容的城市里，"村 BA"、国际水彩艺术季、音乐节等活动承载了人们对美好生活的向往，是乡村旅游与乡土文化、人民精神需求有机结合的体现，也是大黄山旅游发展的最好吸引物。

长三角一体化高质量发展

推动长三角一体化高质量发展是重大的国家战略。近年来，安徽省牢牢抓住这个战略机遇，取得了一系列成就。作为安徽省南部门户的黄山市紧扣"一体化"和"高质量"，推动与沪苏浙全方位、深层次链接，合作机制进一步健全、合作领域进一步拓展、合作成果进一步深化，取得了重要的阶段性成效。

长三角中的安徽

长三角，是长江三角洲的简称，包括上海、江苏、浙江、安徽三省一市，是中国经济版图中最活跃、创新能力最强的区域之一。长三角地区拥有发达的交通网络、雄厚的产业实力和较高的对外开放水平，为区

Genette Rogers, "I am absolutely fascinated. It is so beautiful and ancient that I can sit here and paint forever."

Baidu and Huangshan jointly created the Spring Music Carnival of 50,000 people, with inheriting intangible cultural heritage and technological experience as the core highlight, and different music types such as folk, rock, hip-hop and pop as the content, which was popular and became the focus of the public concern.

In this friendly, beautiful, open and inclusive city, "village basketball game", international watercolor art season, music festival and other activities carry people's yearning for a better life, and are the embodiment of the organic combination of rural tourism, local culture and people's spiritual needs, and also the best attraction of the "Grand Huangshan" tourism development.

The High-Quality Integrated Development of the Yangtze River Delta

It is a major national strategy to promote the integrated development of the Yangtze River Delta. In recent years, Anhui Province has firmly seized this strategic opportunity and made a series of achievements. As the gateway to the southern part of Anhui Province, Huangshan City closely follows the "integration" and "high-quality", and promotes the all-round and deep link with Shanghai, Jiangsu and Zhejiang. The cooperation mechanism between the four provinces has

迎客天下
YING KE TIAN XIA

域内产业集群协调发展提供条件。例如一辆新能源汽车能够在 4 小时车程内解决所需配套零部件供应。这标志着已形成体现现代化产业体系特征的"4 小时产业圈"。

安徽省是长三角经济区的重要组成部分，是参与"一带一路"建设的重要省份，是被长三角一体化发展、长江经济带高质量发展、中部地区高质量发展等国家战略叠加覆盖的省份。安徽省以创新为核心，不断提升配置资金、技术、人才和人口等要素资源的能力和水平，积极主动地将生态资源转化为绿色发展，全面打造新兴产业。2023 年安徽省集成电路产量增长 1 倍以上，柔性显示产业产值增长 1.9 倍，装备制造产业营收突破万亿元，新材料产业产值突破 5200 亿元。同时，安徽省持续专注于提高民生水平。安徽以社会保障卡为载体建立居民服务一卡通办。在群众最关注、感受最直接的医疗领域，安徽已获批 9 个国家区域医疗中心项目，其中大部分项目与沪苏浙医院携手共建。

在长三角一体化高质量发展的浪潮中，安徽省实现了"总量居中、人均靠后"向"总量靠前、人均居中"的跨越发展，全省经济总量跻身全国前十。

黄山："南桥头堡"

黄山茶林场成立于 1965 年 10 月，是上海市飞地。走进茶林场，一幢幢典型海派风格的建筑，一块块辨

been further improved, the areas of cooperation have been further expanded, and the cooperation results have been further deepened, and important initial results have been achieved.

Anhui Province in the Yangtze River Delta

The Yangtze River Delta, which includes Shanghai City, and Jiangsu, Zhejiang and Anhui provinces, is one of the most active and innovative regions in China's economic landscape. The Yangtze River Delta region has a developed transportation network, a strong industrial strength and a high level of opening-up, which provides conditions for the coordinated development of industrial clusters in the region. For example, a new energy vehicle can obtain the supply of supporting parts within 4 hours' drive. This marks the formation of a "4-hour industrial circle" reflecting the characteristics of the modern industrial system.

Anhui Province is a crucial constituent of the Yangtze River Delta Economic Zone and a significant participant in the Belt and Road Initiative. It is also a province encompassed by national strategies such as the integration of the Yangtze River Delta, high-quality development of the Yangtze River Economic Belt, and high-quality development of central China. With innovation as the core, Anhui Province continuously improves the ability and level of allocating capital, technology, talent and population resources, actively transforms ecological resources into green development, and builds emerging industries in an all-round way. In 2023, the output of integrated circuits in Anhui Province increased

迎客天下
YING KE TIAN XIA

识度很高的上海门牌，一个个上海里弄的小区名……极具上海特色。20世纪六七十年代，大量上海知青和他们的家属曾在这里开垦荒地、产茶育林，兴修水利，修建公路，建设水力发电站，解决了生活照明和鲜茶叶加工的用电问题。来自上海的知青最多时有1万多人，他们在这生活、奋斗，为这里留下了"安徽小上海"的美誉，也将两地群众紧密相连。

教育家、思想家、伟大的民主主义战士陶行知出生于黄山，这里也是他接受启蒙教育、走上教育救国道路的出发地。南京，见证了陶行知的青春岁月，更承载了他的教育理想。抗日战争时期，由陶行知担任校长的私立南京安徽中学紧急迁至黄山屯溪，成立徽州分校。如今，宁黄两地保持着密切频繁的文旅交流和商贸合作。

一条新安江，流经皖浙两省的高山与田野，哺育流域内的千万儿女。更值得一提的是，新安江不仅是长三角下游地区重要的战略水源地，也是华东地区重要的生态安全屏障。江水连心，接轨长三角，一直是黄山的战略部署之一。

黄山市与上海、浙江、南京渊源深厚、交往密切。如今，10条高铁汇聚皖南，黄山是继上海、杭州、南京、合肥之后长三角第五大高铁枢纽。2024年6月15日，首条长三角列车环线开行，单向行驶里程超过

by more than double, the output value of flexible display industry increased 1.9 times, the revenue of equipment manufacturing industry exceeded one trillion yuan, and the output value of new materials industry exceeded 520 billion yuan. At the same time, Anhui Province continues to focus on improving people's livelihood. Anhui Province has established one-card office of resident service by social security cards. In the medical field, which the people are most concerned about and feel the most directly, Anhui Province has been approved for 9 national regional medical center projects, most of which are jointly built with hospitals in Shanghai, Jiangsu and Zhejiang.

In the wave of the high-quality integrated development of the Yangtze River Delta, Anhui Province has realized the leap development from "in the middle of the total and in the lowest per capita" to "top in the total and in the middle per capita", and the economic aggregate of the province ranks among the top ten in China.

Huangshan: "the South Bridgehead"

Huangshan Tea Farm, an enclave of Shanghai, was founded in October 1965. Stepping into the tea farm, one will get a view of blocks of typical Shanghai style buildings, pieces of highly recognizable Shanghai doors, the names of Shanghai lane neighborhood... these elements are the characteristics of Shanghai. In the 1960s and 1970s, a large number of Shanghai educated youth and their families worked here to cultivate wasteland and cultivate water conservancy, roads and

迎客天下
YING KE TIAN XIA

新安江夜景（胡健然　摄）
Night view of Xin'an River (Photo by Hu Jianran)

1200 公里，全程 8 小时 9 分钟，横跨沪苏浙皖，串联起长三角地区的上海、南京、合肥、杭州、黄山这 5 座枢纽城市。这里注定是安徽省融入长三角一体化发展国家战略的"南桥头堡"，是长三角一体化发展的重

hydropower stations, which solved the problem of electricity consumption for living lighting and fresh tea processing. At the most, there were more than 10,000 educated youth from Shanghai living and struggling here. It left the reputation of "Small Shanghai in Anhui Province" and closely connected the people of the two places.

Tao Xingzhi, an educator, a thinker and a great democratic soldier, was born in Huangshan City, which is also the starting point for him to receive enlightenment education and embark on the road of saving the country through education. Nanjing had witnessed Tao Xingzhi's youth and carried his educational ideal. During the Anti-Japanese War, the private Nanjing-Anhui Middle School, with Tao Xingzhi as the principal, was urgently moved to Tunxi, Huangshan, and established the Huizhou branch school. Nowadays, Nanjing and Huangshan have maintained close and frequent cultural and tourism exchanges and business cooperation.

Xin'an River flows through the mountains and fields of Anhui and Zhejiang provinces, feeding tens of thousands of children in the basin. It is more worth mentioning that the Xin'an River is not only an important strategic water source in the lower reaches of the Yangtze River Delta, but also an important ecological security barrier in East China. Connecting with the Yangtze River Delta, Xin'an River has been one of the strategic deployment of Huangshan.

Huangshan City has deep ties and close contacts

迎客天下
YING KE TIAN XIA

要参与者、积极推动者和直接受益者，谱写了中国式现代化的长三角－黄山篇章。

黄山："国际会客厅"

黄山市紧紧抓住重大系列外交外事活动带来的机遇，持续放大"屯溪倡议"溢出效应，主动服务国家总体外交，积极打造"国际会客厅"，打好山水牌、人文牌、国际牌、乡村牌，着力讲好中国故事黄山篇章。

国际屯溪

迎客松张开双臂，热情欢迎世界各地的朋友。在美丽黄山脚下的屯溪，一场场大国主场外交活动密集举行。

2022年3月31日，第三次阿富汗邻国外长会在屯溪举行。中国、伊朗、巴基斯坦、俄罗斯、塔吉克斯坦、土库曼斯坦、乌兹别克斯坦七国外长或高级代表出席会议。习近平主席书面致辞。联合国秘书长古特雷斯发表视频致辞。会议发表了《第三次阿富汗邻国外长会联合声明》和《阿富汗邻国关于支持阿富汗经济重建及务实合作的屯溪倡议》。这两份文件体现了邻国的共同政治立场，决定在人道援助、互联互通、经贸领域、农业发展、能源电力、能力建设等重点领域向阿富汗提供实质性支持。

with Shanghai, Zhejiang and Nanjing. Today, 10 high-speed railways converge in the southern Anhui, and Huangshan City is the fifth largest high-speed railway hub in the Yangtze River Delta after Shanghai, Hangzhou, Nanjing and Hefei. On June 15, 2024, the first train ring line in the Yangtze River Delta started, with a one-way mileage of more than 1,200 kilometers for 8 hours and 9 minutes, spanning Shanghai, Jiangsu, Zhejiang and Anhui, connecting the five hub cities—Shanghai, Nanjing, Hefei, Hangzhou and Huangshan in the Yangtze River Delta region. It is destined to be "the south bridgehead" for Anhui Province to integrate into the national strategy of the integrated development of the Yangtze River Delta, and is an important participant, active promoter and direct beneficiary of the integrated development of the Yangtze River Delta. Huangshan City has written its own chapter of the Chinese modernization Yangtze River Delta.

Huangshan: "the International Meeting Room"

Huangshan City firmly seizes the opportunities brought by a series of major diplomatic activities, continues to amplify the spillover effect of "the Tunxi Initiative", actively serves the country's overall diplomacy, and actively builds "the international meeting room". With landscape, culture, internationalization and countryside as the starting point, it will focus on telling the Huangshan chapter of China story.

迎客天下
YING KE TIAN XIA

2023 RCEP 黄山论坛倡议（樊成柱　摄）
2023 RCEP Huangshan Forum Initiative (Photo by Fan Chengzhu)

　　2023 RCEP 地方政府暨友城合作（黄山）论坛6月7日至10日在黄山市屯溪区盛大举行。本次论坛以"区域合作　共赢未来"为主题，通过"线上＋线下"相结合的方式，包括开幕式暨主旨报告、RCEP 成员国友城对话会、RCEP 成员国经贸和开发区合作恳谈会、RCEP 成员国文旅产业合作恳谈会、生命健康分论坛、文旅商品展览展示等多个活动。与会嘉宾围绕深化政府间友好交往，经贸、文旅产业发展，生命健康和医疗卫生领域等多个主题进行深入探讨，为如何全面有

International Tunxi

The Guest-Greeting Pine extending its arms warmly welcomes friends from all over the world. At the foot of the beautiful Mount Huangshan, in Tunxi, diplomatic activities are held intensively.

The third foreign ministers' meeting among the neighboring countries of Afghanistan was held in Tunxi on March 31, 2022. Foreign ministers or senior representatives of seven countries, namely China, Iran, Pakistan, Russia, Tajikistan, Turkmenistan and Uzbekistan, attended the meeting. President Xi Jinping sent a congratulatory message to the meeting. UN Secretary-General Antonio Guterres delivered remarks via video link. The meeting issued the *Joint Statement of the Third Foreign Ministers' Meeting Among the Neighboring Countries of Afghanistan* and the *Tunxi Initiative of the Neighboring Countries of Afghanistan on Supporting Economic Reconstruction and Practical Cooperation with Afghanistan*. The two documents reflect the common political position of neighboring countries and have decided to provide substantive support to Afghanistan in key areas such as humanitarian assistance, connectivity, economic and trade fields, agricultural development, energy and electricity, and capacity building.

The RCEP Local Government and Friendship City Cooperation (Huangshan) Forum was held in Tunxi District, Huangshan City, from June 7 to 10, 2023. Themed "Deepening Regional Cooperation, Creating Win-Win

迎客天下
YING KE TIAN XIA

效实施 RCEP 建言献策，助力更多企业更大范围、更宽领域、更深层次参与到 RCEP 区域经贸合作中去。

国际研学

2023 年 10 月，由商务部主办、上海商学院商务部国际商务官员研修基地承办的发展中国家企业国际化经营能力研修班在中共黄山市委党校（黄山市行政学院）开展实践教学考察交流活动。

研修班学员来自阿尔巴尼亚、约旦、尼日利亚、巴勒斯坦、卢旺达、斯里兰卡、特立尼达和多巴哥、委内瑞拉等 8 个国家。来自各国的学员在世界文化遗产地、中国画里乡村、祁红茶制作企业、啤酒制造企业、历史文化名村、特色创意小镇等开展实践教学。他们通过切身体验与实践，感受到了中国式现代化的黄山成就。

2024 年 2 月，中共黄山市委党校（黄山市行政学院）承办了外交学院瑙鲁留学生培训班的访学活动。一位学员表示："走在这座城市的大街小巷，我们都能听到中国人一声亲切的'你好'，这其实可以感受到中国源远流长的文化。他们以礼貌而著称。"

2024 年 4 月，由商务部主办、上海商学院商务部国际商务官员研修基地承办的马拉维发展与治理研修班走进市委党校，开展实践教学考察交流活动。来自马拉维议会、外交部、总统和内阁办公室等多个部门

Future", the forum included various activities such as a keynote report, a roundtable dialogue involving RCEP member cities, a life and health sub-forum, as well as cultural and tourism exhibitions. The participants had in-depth discussions on deepening the friendly exchanges between governments, economy, trade, cultural and tourism industry development, life, health and medical and healthcare, and made suggestions on how to fully and effectively implement RCEP, and help more enterprises participate in RCEP regional economic and trade cooperation in a wider range, in a wider field and in a deeper level.

International Research

In October 2023, the seminar on international operation ability of enterprises in developing countries, sponsored by the Ministry of Commerce and organized by the International Business Officials Training Base of the Ministry of Shanghai School of Commerce, held a practical teaching inspection and exchange activity in the Party School of Huangshan Municipal Committee of CPC (Huangshan Academy of Governance).

The participants were from eight countries, including Albania, Jordan, Nigeria, Palestine, Rwanda, Sri Lanka, Trinidad and Tobago and Venezuela. They carried out practical teaching in world cultural heritage sites, Chinese painting villages, Qihong tea production enterprises, beer manufacturing enterprises, historical and cultural villages, characteristic creative towns. Through personal experience and practice, they felt the achievements of Chinese modernization.

迎客天下
YING KE TIAN XIA

的 27 名学员，在"国际会客厅"共同体验了一场山水名胜与人文风韵交汇、传统文化与现代发展共进的"黄山之旅"。活动期间，商务部国际商务官员实践教学基地揭牌仪式在中共黄山市委党校（黄山市行政学

学员正在了解红茶制作工艺（胡健然 摄）

Students are learning about the process of making black tea (Photo by Hu Jianran)

In February 2024, in the Party School of the Huangshan Municipal Committee of the CPC (Huangshan Academy of Governance) hosted the visiting study activities for Nauru international students in China Foreign Affairs University. A student said, "Walking in the streets of the city, we can hear 'hello' from the Chinese people, which makes us actually feel the long-standing Chinese culture. They are known for their politeness."

In April 2024, the Malawi Development and Governance Seminar, sponsored by the Ministry of Commerce and undertaken by the International Business Officials Training Base of the Ministry of Shanghai School of Commerce, entered in the Party school to carry out practical teaching investigation and exchange activities. 27 students from Malawi's parliament, the Ministry of Foreign Affairs, the President and the Cabinet Office experienced a "journey to Huangshan" where the landscape and cultural charm converge, and the traditional culture advances alongside modern development. During the event, the opening ceremony of the practice teaching base for international business officials of the Ministry of Commerce was held in the Party school, and it became one of the practice teaching bases for international business officials of the Ministry of Commerce.

On June 22, 2024, 28 students from the Belt and Road National Tourism and Hotel Management Seminar of Shanghai School of Commerce visited Huangshan. A student from Brazil said at the symposium, "The four-day

迎客天下
YING KE TIAN XIA

院）举行，市委党校成为商务部国际商务官员实践教学基地之一。

2024年6月22日，上海商学院"一带一路"国家旅游与酒店管理研修班的28名学员来黄山考察。一位来自巴西的学员在座谈会上发言说："历时四天的黄山游学历程，让我了解到了黄山发展的轨迹，这对我来说是意味深远的，因为它改变了我生活的某一部分。在座的很多同学跟我有同样的想法。"

中共黄山市委党校（黄山市行政学院）聚焦黄山"国际会客厅"建设，充分发挥国际商务官员实践教学基地的窗口作用，全方位、立体式展现中国式现代化的黄山实践，在国际培训中更好展示黄山、推介黄山。

国际交流

2023环黄山国际公路自行车赛经国际自行车联盟（UCI，法语Union Cycliste Internationale）批准，已获得国际自行车联盟认证（UCI2.2级），纳入奥运积分体系。

2023环黄山国际公路自行车赛7月21日至23日在安徽省黄山市举办。来自28个国家和地区的18支UCI注册职业车队的108名选手骑行穿越黄山、太平湖、新安江、宏村、呈坎、徽州古城等著名人文自然景观。

赛事在赛道设置上独具匠心。共设环黄山主题赛、

study tour in Huangshan has taught me the trajectory of the development of Huangshan, which is profound to me, because it has changed a part of my life. Many students here share the same idea with me."

The Party School of the Huangshan Municipal Committee of the CPC (Huangshan Academy of Governance) will focus on the construction of "the international meeting room" in Huangshan, give full play to the window role of the practice teaching base of international business officials, show the practice of Chinese modernization in an all-round and three-dimensional way, and better display and promote Huangshan in the international training.

International Communication

The 2023 Tour of Huangshan International Road Cycling Race has been approved by the International Cycling Union (UCI, Union Cycliste Internationale in France). It has been certified by the International Cycling Union (UCI 2.2) and included in the Olympic points system.

The 2023 Tour of Huangshan International Road Cycling Race was held in Huangshan City, Anhui Province from July 21 to 23. 108 athletes from 18 UCI registered professional teams from 28 countries and regions rode through Huangshan, Taiping Lake, Xin'an River, Hongcun, Chengkan, Huizhou Ancient City and other famous cultural and natural landscapes.

The race is unique in the track setting. There are three stages: the Huangshan Tour Theme Race, the Landscape of

湖光山色骑行赛、城市沿江绕圈赛三个赛段，线路包含山地、丘陵、平路等类型，考验车手的综合能力，总距离362公里。赛事进行期间，人们还可以通过集市品尝安徽特色美食、感受安徽非遗魅力，在体验骑行乐趣的同时丰富了环黄山赛的独特文化内涵，这让国际友人感受到了深厚的文化底蕴。更值得一提的是，本次赛事注入了智慧科技理念，设立赛事AI形象推广大使来推介赛事、宣传黄山。

从开放中走来的黄山，正以更加自信、更加开放的胸襟面向世界，用更加动人、更加精彩的黄山故事展示中国式现代化的实践成就。

Lakes and Mountain Cycling Race and the City Circle Race along the River. The routes include mountains, hills, flat roads and other types, which test the comprehensive ability of the riders, with a total distance of 362 kilometers. During the event, people can also taste the special food of Anhui and feel the charm of Anhui intangible cultural heritage through the market. While experiencing the fun of cycling, the unique cultural connotation of the Huangshan Tour Race is enriched, which makes international friends feel the profound cultural heritage. What is more worth mentioning is that this event has injected the concept of intelligent science and technology, and set up the event AI image promotion ambassador to promote the event and Huangshan City.

Coming from the opening-up, Huangshan is facing the world with a more confident and open mind, and showing the practical achievements of Chinese modernization with more moving and wonderful Huangshan stories.

后 记

本书是中央党校(国家行政学院)中国式现代化研究中心和中央党校出版集团国家行政学院出版社策划出版的"中国式现代化的故事"丛书之一,是中共黄山市委党校(黄山市行政学院)认真贯彻落实习近平总书记关于"讲好中国故事,传播好中国声音,展示真实、立体、全面的中国"等重要讲话指示精神,扎实开展对外交流工作的又一成果。

中国式现代化的黄山生动实践中,方方面面的案例俯首可得、举不胜举,本书通过多个故事,以小切口、微视角展示黄山儿女谱写中国式现代化黄山篇章的奋斗和成就。故事虽小,也许不能完整、准确代表黄山儿女贯彻新发展理念、谱写中国式现代化黄山篇章的实践探索,但希望故事背后的逻辑和道理可以带给人们诸多启示;故事虽微,也许不能

Epilogue

This book is one of the series of books "The Story of Chinese Modernization" planned and published by the Chinese Modernization Research Center of Party School of Central Committee of CPC (National Academy of Governance) and the National Academy of Governance Press, Party School of Central Committee of CPC Press Group. Meanwhile, it is one of the new achievements of the Party School of Huangshan Municipal Committee of CPC (Huangshan Academy of Governance, hereinafter referred to as Huangshan Party School) in undertaking foreign exchange and communication steadily by conscientiously implementing the important instructions of President Xi Jinping on "Telling the China's stories well, making the voice of China heard, and presenting a true, multi-dimensional, and panoramic view of China to the world".

The vivid practices of Chinese modernization in Huangshan are abundant in numerous cases on all fronts. Taking a series of stories as small angles of view, this book demonstrates the endeavour and accomplishment of Huangshan in writing its own chapter on Chinese modernization. The stories are tiny and may not completely reflect the practical exploration of implementing new development philosophy and writing Huangshan chapter of Chinese modernization by Huangshan people. However, we hope that the logic and reasoning behind these stories bring the readers certain

系统、全面反映中国式现代化建设的黄山成就，但希望大家能感受到黄山山水优美、文化灿烂、生态优质、特产丰饶、区位优越。新时代的黄山正以国际化视野、世界级标准，推动高品质的资源加快形成高端供给，为大黄山世界级休闲度假康养旅游目的地建设注入强劲动能。

本书由中共黄山市委党校（黄山市行政学院）的一批中青年教师撰写。本书由理论研究室聂涛负责全书统稿，各章撰写分工如下：第一章由陈欣撰写并翻译成英文，第二章由方凯丰撰写并翻译成英文，第三章由毛新红、罗丹、钟俊撰写并翻译成英文，第四章由凌蔚强、窦剑撰写并翻译成英文，第五章由梅俊撰写并翻译成英文，第六章由吴咏梅撰写并翻译成英文，第七章由胡健然撰写并翻译成英文。全书英文部分由龚岱辰进行总核对。感谢各位作者的倾力付出。

黄山市人大常委会副主任、中共黄山市委党校（黄山市行政学院）常务副校（院）长卢邦生自始至终关心、推动着本书的编写、出版。副校（院）长邹剑海、倪文华对本书的编写作了很多协调和组织工作。教育长程泉民多次主持召开咨询会，确定了本书的主题内容、篇章结构、风格体例、写作要求。校（院）教研室、理论研究室等部门承担了相关的组织协调工作。黄山日报社在图片资料提供上给予了支持，中共安徽省委

inspiration. The stories are micro and may not comprehensively reveal Huangshan's achievements in the construction of Chinese modernization. Nevertheless, we anticipate that the readers sense that Huangshan has beautiful landscapes, splendid culture, high-quality ecology, rich specialties and superior location. In the new era, the "Grand Huangshan" is advancing with a global perspective and world-class standards, aiming to expedite the transformation of high-quality resources into premium offerings and infuse robust momentum into the development of the Grand Huangshan world-class leisure and healthcare tourism destination.

This book was written by a group of young and middle-aged lecturers from Huangshan Party School. This book was compiled by Nie Tao from the Theoretical Research Department, and the division for each chapter is as follows: Chapter 1 was written and translated by Chen Xin, Chapter 2 was written and translated by Fang Kaifeng, Chapter 3 was written and translated by Mao Xinhong, Luo Dan and Zhong Jun, Chapter 4 was written and translated by Ling Weiqiang and Dou Jian, Chapter 5 was written and translated by Mei Jun, Chapter 6 was written and translated by Wu Yongmei, Chapter 7 was written and translated by Hu Jianran, and the entire English text was verified by Gong Daichen. All of your dedication is deeply appreciated.

Lu Bangsheng, Deputy Director of the Standing Committee of the Huangshan Municipal People's Congress and Executive Vice Chancellor of Huangshan Party School, has always been concerned about and promoted the preparation and publication of this book. Vice Chancellors Zou Jianhai and Ni Wenhua have done a lot of coordination and organization work for the writing of this book. Education director Cheng Quanmin has presided over multiple consultation meetings to determine the theme, structure,

党校（安徽行政学院）国际合作部对本书写作进行了精心指导，国家行政学院出版社作了细致的编辑工作。在此一并感谢！

　　编写供对外交流使用的双语读物，是中共黄山市委党校（黄山市行政学院）的首次尝试与探索，由于时间较紧，资料受限，加之作者水平有限，疏漏和不足之处在所难免，敬请各位读者批评指正。

编者
2024 年 10 月

style, and writing requirements of this book. The Teaching and Research Department, the Theoretical Research Department and other departments of the school have undertaken the relevant organizational and coordination work. Huangshan Daily gives support in providing picture materials. The International Cooperation Department of the Party School of Anhui Provincial Committee of CPC (Anhui Academy of Governance) gives careful guidance to this book, and the National Academy of Governance Press has done careful editing work. Here, we would like to extend our sincere gratitude to you all!

It is the first attempt and exploration of Huangshan Party School to compile bilingual readings for foreign communication. Due to constraints in time and materials, and limited competence of the authors, drawbacks and omissions might be unavoidable. Cordially, we look forward to your criticism and correction.

Editorial Board
October 2024

图书在版编目（CIP）数据

迎客天下：中国式现代化的黄山故事：汉英对照 / 中共黄山市委党校（黄山市行政学院）编著 . -- 北京：国家行政学院出版社，2024.11. --（"中国式现代化的故事"丛书 / 张占斌主编）. -- ISBN 978-7-5150-2957-3

Ⅰ. D675.43

中国国家版本馆 CIP 数据核字第 2024B4R867 号

书　　名	迎客天下——中国式现代化的黄山故事 YING KE TIANXIA——ZHONGGUOSHI XIANDAIHUA DE HUANGSHAN GUSHI
作　　者	中共黄山市委党校（黄山市行政学院）　编著
统筹策划	胡　敏　刘韫劼　王　莹
责任编辑	王　莹　孔令慧
责任校对	许海利
责任印刷	吴　霞
出版发行	国家行政学院出版社 （北京市海淀区长春桥路 6 号　100089）
综 合 办	（010）68928887
发 行 部	（010）68928866
经　　销	新华书店
印　　刷	北京新视觉印刷有限公司
版　　次	2024 年 11 月北京第 1 版
印　　次	2024 年 11 月北京第 1 次印刷
开　　本	145 毫米 × 210 毫米　32 开
印　　张	7.75
字　　数	125 千字
定　　价	50.00 元

本书如有印装问题，可联系调换。联系电话：（010）68929022